# Guide to North Cyprus

# Guide to
# North Cyprus

## 2nd edition

**Diana Darke**

Bradt Publications, UK
The Globe Pequot Press Inc, USA

First published in 1993 by Bradt Publications.
Second edition published by Bradt Publications,
41 Nortoft Road, Chalfont St Peter, Bucks SL9 0LA, England
Published in the USA by The Globe Pequot Press Inc, 6 Business Park Road,
PO Box 833, Old Saybrook, Connecticut 06475-0833

The author and publishers have made every effort to ensure the accuracy of the
information in this book at the time of going to press. However, they cannot accept any
responsibility for any loss, injury or inconvenience resulting from the use of information
contained in this guide.

**British Library Cataloguing in Publication Data**
A catalogue record for this book is available from the British Library
ISBN 1 898323 27 5

**Library of Congress Cataloging-in-Publication Data**
Darke, Diana.
    Guide to North Cyprus / Diana Darke. — 2nd ed.
        p. cm — (Bradt guides)
    Includes index.
    ISBN 1-56440-819-1
    1. Cyprus, Northern—Guidebooks. I. Title. II. Series
DS54.95.N67D37 1995
915.69304′4—dc20                                    95-17759
                                                    CIP

**Cover photos** *Front:* Kyrenia Castle from the harbour (Alan Süleyman)
*Back:* Sandal mosaic, Ayia Trias (Sean Hignett)
**Illustrations** Rebecca de Mendonça
**Maps** *Covers:* Steve Munns
*Others:* Patti Taylor from originals compiled by the author

Typeset from the author's disc by Patti Taylor, London NW10 1JR
Printed and bound in Great Britain by The Guernsey Press Co Ltd

## DEDICATION

For Chloë and Max

## ACKNOWLEDGEMENTS

The author would like to thank Metin Münir, Ergün Olgun, Augusta Rieber, Kitty Stubbs, Alma Taylor and Luitgard Hauer for their help in making the preparation of this book possible.

Many thanks are also due to Adil Korel, Tourism Counsellor at the London TRNC Tourist Office, for his great patience in so helpfully answering my queries.

Special thanks are due to Neil Memmott, Mike and Ann Edwards, Mr I Morkunas, Altan Houssein of the Soli Inn, Anita and Tony Woods, Gillian Shipton, Don Moar and Sam Hignett for their kind and informative letters which have been most helpful in preparing this second edition.

## ABOUT THE AUTHOR

Diana Darke first became interested in the Near East when she read Arabic at Oxford. For the last eighteen years she has lived, worked and travelled extensively in Turkey and the Arab world, initially with the Foreign Office, then as an Arabic consultant. Work and pleasure have taken her to both sides of Cyprus on many occasions.

Her travel writing career began with the Discovery Guides to *Aegean and Mediterranean Turkey* and *Eastern Turkey and the Black Sea Coast* (Michael Haag/Immel), now in their third editions. Since then she has written a *Discovery Guide to Jordan and the Holy Land* and three new guides to Turkey and Tunisia for the AA. She is married with two children.

# CONTENTS

# FOREWORD

The northern Turkish part of Cyprus — 37% of the island — is rarely visited. No one denies that when the island was divided in 1974, the Turks took the more beautiful and fertile region, but while holidaymakers jostle for beach space at Paphos and Limassol, it's a case of spot the tourist at Kyrenia and Famagusta. The Greek Cypriots are skilful political lobbyists and have since 1974 conducted an effective boycott of the north, presenting it as 'occupied and inaccessible'. They have done a good job, for only an initiated few have been to see for themselves. These have tended to become loyal devotees returning each year to enjoy the wealth of sites and relaxing atmosphere. The Greek Cypriots have also done a good job of rebuilding the tourist industry in the south, but in doing so have disfigured the landscape with concrete high rise and fast food restaurants. Less commercially minded than their southern counterparts, the Turkish Cypriots hatched few ambitious development projects, and were in any event starved of the international finance needed to carry them out. In the north, family investment in a dozen or so chalets set round a pool, offering local cuisine, has been much more the style. Circumstances have therefore conspired, from the visitor's point of view, to keep North Cyprus as probably the most unspoilt corner in the Mediterranean.

Prices in North Cyprus are the among lowest in the Mediterranean, with a meal for two plus wine costing £10-12 and car hire £12 a day. The pace of life is gentle and relaxed with no traffic jams or queues. Turkish Cypriots are friendly and hospitable and do not as a rule hassle or pester visitors. Petty crime rates are very low and the environment is safe and pollution free. There are daily flights from the UK, and tourism is expanding slowly under the aegis of two centre holidays with Turkey. This makes a virtue out of the necessity of touching down at Istanbul or Izmir, a consequence of non-recognition by any country except Turkey.

The political status of the north is an emotive subject for both Greek and Turkish Cypriots, and no guide book would presume to try and analyse the rights and wrongs of the question. The 'Chronology' in the Background section attempts to summarise what happened when, and interested readers will no doubt pursue their enquiries and make up their own minds. The political situation has, ironically, worked in the tourist's favour, by making North Cyprus into a forgotten corner where the Mediterranean of 20 years ago can still be recaptured.

Since 1974, descriptions of the north have been relegated to the back few pages of travel guides covering the whole island. Here it is given the comprehensive coverage it deserves. The practical information section includes full details of hotels, restaurants and beaches.

## Star ratings

A starring system is used throughout the book to highlight places of special interest: *** means 'not to be missed', ** means 'merits a detour', * means 'noteworthy'. At the start of each site description, introductory paragraphs summarise the pros and cons, while detailed timings and distances facilitate planning.

The policy on place names has been to use the foreign version where it is well-known, as in Kyrenia, Famagusta and Nicosia, and otherwise to use the current Turkish, with the former Greek ones in brackets. An appendix decoding the two sets of names is to be found at the back.

Chapter One

# General Information

## BACKGROUND

### Outline

Within its tiny boundaries, Cyprus offers a microcosm of history. Just as Constantinople was always a bridge, so Cyprus was always a stepping stone, where culture after culture left its footprints. Scarcely 224km (140 miles) long and 96km (60 miles) wide, the island has an unrivalled mix and concentration of landscape, history and culture, and with 768km (480 miles) of coastline, the sea and a beach are always close by.

**Turkey is nearest neighbour**

Turkey is its nearest neighbour, just 64km (40 miles) away, followed by Syria 96km (60 miles) distant. It is 400km (250 miles) to Egypt and 480km (300 miles) to the nearest Greek island.

In the current division, the Turkish sector is undoubtedly the more beautiful. The fact that, pre-1974, 80% of Cyprus' hotels were in the Kyrenia and Famagusta areas, shows only too clearly where the tourist potential of the island always lay. The Greek Cypriots energetically set about rebuilding the south, and with the help of foreign aid and investment have now succeeded in developing Paphos, Limassol and Larnaca to be their new resort centres.

The Turkish north, which proclaimed itself the independent Turkish Republic of North Cyprus (TRNC) in 1983, is still not recognised by any country other than Turkey, and has thus been denied foreign finance. Neglect set in and tourism stagnated.

**Growing confidence**

In recent years, however, Turkish Cypriots who left in the '70s have been returning, mainly from Britain and Australia and, increasingly confident in the status quo of partition, are investing their savings in small but well-planned tourist developments. The north is beginning to stir.

## Chronology of Cyprus

There is no specific historical section in this guide, since historical background is woven into the text as and when appropriate. For an overview therefore, the following detailed chronology is provided as a handy reference and summary.

**6000-2500BC** Neolithic settlements. Earliest yet found is Khirokitia near Larnaca 5800BC. Beehive huts of stone.

**2500-2300BC** Chalcolithic period. Discovery of copper on island led to growth in trade.

**1st Bronze Age** (2300-1900BC). Contemporary with early Egyptian dynasties and Minoan civilisations of Crete. Cyprus inhabited by people identical to those found in Central Europe, Asia Minor and Syria.

**2000BC** Enkomi, near Famagusta, major trading centre in copper, becomes capital of Alassia (as Cyprus was then called).

**2nd Bronze Age** (1900-1500BC). Contemporary with middle Egyptian dynasties, Myceneans and Phoenicians colonising the Mediterranean. Cyprus paid tribute to them, but only the Phoenicians and Greeks colonised and left settlements. The Egyptians never occupied. Greek city states of Salamis, Soli, Marion, Curium and Paphos. Cult of Aphrodite introduced. No political link with Greece, as settlers were always breakaways from the mainland, exiles or entrepreneurs wishing to set up a new life in a different land.

**1200BC** Phoenician King Hiram of Tyre invades and gathers tribute. Phoenicians rule Cyprus. Main Phoenician settlement at Kition near Larnaca.

**725-575BC** Assyrian rulers. Sargon to Nebuchadnezzar. Cyprus joins with them in wars against Egyptians.

**525-425BC** Persian rulers including Darius and Xerxes. Cypriots join them in campaigns against Egyptians and Greeks.

**First native ruler**

**411-374BC** Evagorus, king of Salamis, first native ruler. Cyprus independent after Persia and Greece sign truce. Evagorus introduces monarchy, Greek coinage and alphabet, Greek culture favoured.

**350-325BC** Persia regains the island after long siege of Salamis.

**335-263BC** Zeno, founder of Stoic philosophy, born at Kition. Only really great name to come out of Cyprus.

**325BC** Alexander the Great. Cypriots were to send ships to Tyre to help lift siege, but sent them to Alexander instead, thus ensuring overthrow of Persians. Cyprus becomes part of Alexander's empire.

**300-50BC** Hellenistic period. From Alexander's death until arrival of Romans, Cyprus ruled from Alexandria, Egypt, first by Ptolemy, Alexander's general, finally by Cleopatra. Arsinoe (Famagusta) built. Fragments of Egyptian granite and statues found at Salamis. Island is united as four districts for first time and flourishes under relatively peaceful conditions.

**50BC-300AD** 450 years of Roman rule. Romans make Cyprus part of the province of Cilicia (southern Turkey), capital Tarsus, ruled by military governor. Roman engineers build roads, harbours, bridges and aqueducts. Prosperity enjoyed.

**45AD** St Paul and St Barnabas arrive at Salamis on first missionary journey. Roman pro-consul converted to Christianity.

**100AD** Under Roman Emperor Trajan, Jews on island (who had fled here to escape Roman persecution in Palestine), massacre 240,000 Cypriots, including St Barnabas, native of Salamis. As a result, Romans expel all Jews from Cyprus.

**125AD** Under Hadrian, climax of Roman monumental art.

**313AD** Emperor Constantine officially recognises Christianity. Most of Cyprus is already Christian by this time.

**325-1191** Rule of Byzantium.

**325-350** Empress Helena, mother of Constantine, visits on return from trip to Jerusalem. Salamis rebuilt as Constantia after severe earthquakes of 4th century.

**Byzantium divides**  **395** Division of Byzantine empire into east and west. Cyprus comes under eastern half, with capital at Constantinople, but is ruled from Antioch in Syria.

**477** Under Emperor Zeno, autocephalic church of Cyprus is granted, with independent Cypriot archbishop. Monastery of St Barnabas built.

**525** Climax of Byzantine art, period of peace and unity.

**650-965** Series of Arab raids at intervals over next 300 years. Salamis destroyed, never rebuilt, many churches pillaged and torn down. Byzantine art stagnates.

**965-1180** Byzantine emperor defeats Arabs and island secure again. Climax of Cypriot Christian art, new churches and monasteries all over island as Cyprus becomes refuge for Christians fleeing from Holy Land as Arab empire expands there. Castles built as defence against possible future Arab raids.

**Second period of self rule**

**1184** Isaac Comnenus, rebel Byzantine prince from Trabzon, arrives on island and proclaims himself Emperor of Cyprus. Rules for seven years in style of despot, but this is only the second time in Cyprus' history when it is independent of a foreign power.

**1191** Richard the Lionheart captures Cyprus on way to Third Crusade.

**1192** Richard sells Cyprus to Knights Templar to raise money for his army. Then sells it to Guy de Lusignan, last king of Jerusalem before Saladin's conquest, as a consolation for Guy's loss of Jerusalem.

**Catholic takeover**

**1192-1489** Norman French occupation under the Lusignan dynasty. Castle and town of Nicosia built under Amaury, Guy's brother. Feudal system created, like kingdom of Jerusalem. Rulers take titles of King of Cyprus and King of Jerusalem (in absentia).

**1225** Byzantine castles of Hilarion, Buffavento and Kantara refortified and elaborated by the Lusignan Crusaders.

**1250** Cathedral of Nicosia built.

**1300** Cathedral of Famagusta built after fall of Acre, last Christian toehold in Holy Land.

**1325** Bellapais Abbey built. Native islanders isolated from new wealth by ruling Catholic French speakers and treated as serfs. Orthodox church persecuted and humiliated, made subject to Rome and the Pope.

**1375-1464** Cyprus under vassalage to Genoa. Island at war and Famagusta is ceded to Genoese as settlement. Rest of the island stays under Lusignans.

**1425** Egyptian Mamelukes pillage towns and weaken Lusignan dynasty.

**1464** Genoese expelled. Last Lusignan king takes Venetian bride, Catherine Cornaro, but both he and his new-born son are murdered, leaving Catherine nominally in control, while Venetian nobles arrange her retirement to Italy.

**1489-1571** Venetian Republic occupation. Fortification of castles at Kyrenia, Famagusta and Nicosia. Dismantling of mountain castles of Hilarion, Buffavento and Kantara to discourage internal uprising.

**1481** Leonardo da Vinci visits, possibly advising on fortification design.

**Turkish rule**

**1571-1878** Three centuries of Turkish rule under the Ottomans. Only resistance offered by Venetian strongholds of Nicosia and Famagusta. Islanders themselves glad to see end of oppressive Venetian rule. Orthodox church recognised again and Archbishopric restored. Feudal system abolished, but heavy taxes imposed, using church as tax collectors.

**1625-1700** Great depopulation of Cyprus. Plagues wipe out over half population.

**1821** Greek Cypriots side with Greece in revolt against Turkish rule. Island's leading churchmen are executed in punishment.

**1869** Suez Canal opens.

**1878-1960** British occupation. British take on administration of the island, ceded from the Ottomans, for its strategic value, to protect their sea route to India via the Suez Canal. In exchange, Britain agrees to help Turkey should Russia attack again.

**1914** Cyprus annexed by Britain when Turkey joins with Germany and Austro-Hungary in World War I.

**1925** Cyprus becomes British Crown Colony.

**1931** First serious riots of Greek Cypriots demanding Enosis, union with Greece.

**1939** Greek Cypriots fight with British in World War II, but remain set on Enosis after war is over. Turkish Cypriots however, want British rule to continue.

**1950** Archbishop Makarios III elected political and spiritual leader. Heads the campaign for Enosis with the support of Greece.

**Civil strife** **1955** Series of bomb attacks, start of violent campaign for Enosis by EOKA (National Organisation of Cypriot Fighters) led by George Grivas, ex-colonel in Greek army, born in Cyprus. Grivas takes name of Dighenis, legendary Cypriot hero, and conducts guerilla warfare from secret hideout in Troodos mountains. Estimated to have 300 men maximum, yet successfully plagues 20,000 British troops and 4,500 police.

**1956** Britain deports Makarios to Seychelles in attempt to quell revolt. Turkish Cypriots used as auxiliaries of British Security Forces, allegedly torturing EOKA captives during British cross-examinations.

**1957** Field Marshal Sir John Harding replaced by civilian governor Sir Hugh Foot in conciliatory move.

**1958** Turkish Cypriots alarmed by British conciliation and begin demands for partition. Inter-communal clashes and attacks on British.

**Third period of self rule** **1960** British, Greek and Turkish governments sign Treaty of Guarantee to provide for independent Cypriot state within the Commonwealth and allowing for retention of two Sovereign Base Areas of Dhekelia and Akrotiri. Under the treaty, each power has the right to take military action in the face of any threat to the constitution. Cyprus truly independent for first time. Archbishop Makarios is first President, Dr Kütchük Vice-President. Both have right of veto.

Turkish Cypriots, who form 18% of population, given 30% of places in government and administration, 40% in army, and separate municipal services in the five major towns.

**1963-1973** Greek Cypriots view constitution as unworkable and propose changes which are rejected by Turkish Cypriots and Turkish government. Intercommunal fighting escalates and UN Peace Keeping Force sent in, but powerless to prevent incidents.

**1974-1976** Military government (*junta*) in Greece supports coup by Greek National Guard to overthrow Makarios. Makarios forced to flee. Puppet regime imposed under Nicos Sampson, former EOKA fighter. Rauf Denktash, Turkish Cypriot leader, calls for joint military action by the UK and Turkey, as guarantors of Cypriot independence, to prevent Greece imposing Enosis. The Turkish prime minister travels to London to persuade the UK to intervene jointly with Turkey, but fails, so Turkey exercises her right under the 1960 Treaty of Guarantee and lands 40,000 troops on the north coast of Cyprus. Turkey describes this invasion as 'a peace operation to restore constitutional order and protect the Turkish Cypriot community'. UN talks break down and Turkish forces are left in control of

**The island divides** 37% of the island. Refugees from both communities cross to respective sides of the *de facto* border. Turks announce Federated State in the north with Denktash as leader. UN Forces stay as buffer between the two zones. Some 20,000 mainland Turks, mainly subsistence farmers, are brought in to settle and work the underpopulated land. Those that stay more than five years are given citizenship of North Cyprus.

**1977** Makarios dies, having been restored as President of Greek Cyprus after 1974. Succeeded by Spyros Kyprianou.

**1983** Turkish Federated State declares itself independent, as Turkish Republic of North Cyprus

(TRNC), still with Denktash as President. New state is not recognised by any country except Turkey.

**1992-1995** UN sponsored talks between the two sides run into the sand, but with a commitment to resume.

## POPULATION

In 1980 the population of the whole island was 625,000. Of these 77% were Greek Cypriots and 18% Turkish Cypriots. 5% were minorities (Armenians, Maronites and British). The Greek Cypriots consider themselves ethnically Greek, tracing their ancestry back to the Mycenean settlements of the 14th century BC. In its early history, the island allied itself with Greece against Persia and against the Arabs, and under the 800 year rule of Byzantium, the independent orthodox church was established on the island.

**Ethnic mix**      The Turkish Cypriots are the descendants of the mainland Turks who stayed behind after the Ottoman conquest, or of settlers who came across from the mainland at that time. They are Muslim, though generally not especially devout. Since the breakdown of the 1960 Constitution they have been self-administered.

The 1990 figures are 600,000 Greek Cypriots in the south, with 160,000 Turkish Cypriots in the north. Post 1974, immigrants were brought in from mainland Turkey, often rural subsistence farmers from eastern Anatolia, to settle in the underpopulated north and work the land. They are thought to number about 50,000 today.

## RELIGION

Turkish Cypriots are Sunni (ie: orthodox) Muslims, but research studies have consistently shown them to be far less practising than their mainland counterparts. Islam is not a dominant force on the island. There are surprisingly few mosques and the call to prayer is rarely heard. Like Turkey, the secular weekend of Saturday/Sunday is used, rather than the Muslim

Friday. Shops and restaurants function as normal during the fasting month of Ramadan.

## EDUCATION

Even before partition, schools were separate for Greek and Turkish Cypriots, though there was a bicommunal school in Nicosia established by the British. In 1971, there were 542 Greek primary and 42 secondary schools, and 166 Turkish primary and 19 secondary schools. Schooling has been much expanded in the north since partition, with 21 colleges and technical schools. The University of the Eastern Mediterranean has been established in Famagusta, of the Near East in Nicosia, and a new one in Lefke. Science, engineering and management are the largest faculties.

English is the language of instruction in all the universities.

In Kyrenia, the private University College of North Cyprus also offers degree courses in Business Administration.

## ECONOMY

**Chaos after partition**

Partition in 1974 resulted in dramatic changes. Some 180,000 Greek Cypriots were rehoused in the south. With aid and investment from abroad, especially in agriculture, construction and tourism, Greek Cyprus made a remarkable recovery and was able to provide near full employment. Some 45,000 Turkish Cypriots were rehoused in the north. 80% of the tourist infrastructure lay in the northern zone and there has been further development. Güzelyurt (Morphou), the market garden of Cyprus, now lies in the north and provides 50% of the TRNC's foreign exchange income, and 50 million tons of the 65 million tons of water in the north.

Though the Greek and Turkish sectors have struggled to survive independently, two areas of cooperation remain: water and electricity. Most of the water reserves are in the Turkish north, and in exchange for water, the Greek south provides electricity to the north. This will shortly change, once Turkish Cyprus completes the building of its own power stations.

Greek Cyprus has now submitted a formal application to join the EEC, anxious not to be excluded from the 1992 market. No new applications will be considered for now, says the EEC, after the influx from eastern Europe. Turkish Cyprus sends 60% of its exports to the EEC, 55% of them to the UK, while only 13% goes to the Arab world. These exports consist of agricultural produce, mainly 'new' potatoes, citrus fruits, olives, tobacco and carobs.

**Inflation**     Since the 1994 devaluations of the Turkish Lira, there has been rampant inflation, making life very difficult for Turkish Cypriots who have no access to foreign currency.

## ATMOSPHERE AND AMBIENCE

The atmosphere in the north is relaxed and friendly. The people are by nature easy going and violent crime is virtually nil. The aggravating hassling of foreigners by street sellers and shop owners, rampant in other parts of the Mediterranean, is blissfully absent here. If you ask for help, it will be offered willingly, but if
**Absence**     you are just strolling and looking, you will be left to
**of hassle**     yourself. Women alone are not propositioned and it is quite safe to walk round after dark. Your privacy is respected and people keep their distance.

Although there are some 26,000 troops from the Turkish army stationed in camps here, they are highly disciplined and under strict instructions to be courteous to foreigners. Should you inadvertently stray into a military area, you will be politely escorted out and redirected. The following areas of interest to tourists are inaccessible military zones:

**Military**     Lambousa, on the coast west of Kyrenia
**zones**     Paleokastro, on Güzelyurt Bay
Ayios Panteleimon Monastery at Çamlıbel
Ayios Chrysostomos Monastery below Buffavento
    castle

Ayios Spiridon, southeast of Ercan airport
Varosha, south of Famagusta
Chrysokava quarries, east of Kyrenia

**Notices**   Notices saying 'No Photography — Military Area' should always be taken seriously.

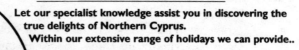

# Chapter Two

# **Practical Information**

## GETTING THERE

**By air**   TRNC's airport for tourist traffic is Ercan (formerly called Tymbou), small, but newly equipped and expanded, situated some 12km (7 miles) east of Nicosia. Scheduled flights by Turkish Airlines (THY) and Cyprus Turkish Airlines (a subsidiary of THY) run at least twice daily from Istanbul. Charter flights direct to Ercan on B373's run daily from Heathrow, Gatwick, Stansted and Manchester by either Sun Express, Istanbul Airlines or Onur Air, and it is possible to mix airlines to suit your own timetable, the cost being determined by the outward flight code. The average return adult fare is £250. All flights to Ercan have to touch down on the Turkish mainland, since TRNC is not recognised by anyone except Turkey. From Europe, the touch down points are usually Istanbul or Izmir, or occasionally Antalya or Dalaman. Passengers for Ercan do not leave the plane, but simply wait a while on the tarmac. From the Turkish mainland itself, there are additional direct flights to Ercan from Ankara, Antalya and Adana. There are about ten flights a week to Ercan from the UK.

Another method for those who do not mind the hassle is to get the cheapest available flight to Istanbul, then buy a return ticket to Ercan from the THY or CTY (Cyprus Turkish Airlines) office at Istanbul. The return excursion fare Istanbul-Ercan is only c. £80, as it is classed as an internal domestic flight. Despite this, all flights to Ercan use the

International Atatürk Airport, rather than the scruffy domestic terminal used for other internal flights. This is a great bonus as any time spent waiting for connections is far more pleasant, Atatürk International Airport being very modern and efficient, with an extensive range of shops. Its restaurant on the upper floor serves good wholesome food at reasonable prices. Flights to Ercan get fairly full, so it is advisable to have reserved in advance, then pay and collect the tickets at Istanbul. Note that while THY accepts VISA cards, CTY, for some reason, accepts no credit cards at all. Payment is in Turkish lira, and the airport banks are always open if you need to change money. Check-in time at Istanbul is two hours ahead of flight time. Duty free allowances on entry are one litre of spirits and 400 cigarettes. The best agents for flights both to Ercan and to Istanbul are Sunquest, 9 Grand Parade, Green Lanes, London N4 1JX tel: 0181-800 8030, fax: 0181-809 6629, and President Holidays, 542 Kingsland Road, London E8 4AH tel: 0171-249 4002, fax: 0171-923 2602.

**By sea**  Car ferries of Turkish Maritime Lines run all the year round from Mersin in southern Turkey to Famagusta. (London agents of TML: Walford Lines Limited, Ibec House, 42-47 Minories, London EC3N 1AE, tel: 0171-480 5621. Famagusta office tel: 3665995/ 3665786.)

In summer, three types of boat also run from Taşucu in southern Turkey to the new harbour at Kyrenia. The fastest is for passengers only and carries 250 people, making the journey daily except Saturdays in two and a half hours. A car ferry runs three times a week in summer, taking six hours, with a capacity of 120 cars and 800 passengers. Both these services are run by Fergün Denizcilik, tel: Kyrenia 8152344/8153377. Finally, there is an old car ferry taking eight hours and carrying 50 cars and 400 passengers, run by Ertürk Denizcilik, tel: Kyrenia 8152308/8152480. Cars can be imported into TRNC without customs duty for up to three months, a permit being issued at the port of entry. The permit can be renewed for up to a year. Vehicles must be accompanied by an insurance certificate valid for TRNC, which can be bought at the port. These ferries can be booked from the UK via Sunquest Holidays or in North Cyprus from most travel agents. Fares are very reasonable.

## Access from Greek Cyprus

From the Greek sector you can travel across into the Turkish north just for the day. You present yourself with passport at the police crossing point beside the Ledra Palace Hotel in Nicosia. There you are 'logged out' by the Greek Cypriot authorities and asked to return before nightfall. This restriction is implemented by the Greek Cypriot authorities, since they do not want visitors to stay the night in 'the illegally occupied zone'.

**Border formalities**

You may take across a private vehicle, registered in your name (not hired) for which you then buy insurance at the Turkish checkpoint. Occasionally, and for indefinite periods, the Greeks suspend the issuing of these permits, as a reprisal against the north if something has offended them, such as an uncompromising statement by Denktash. The situation varies according to the political climate, and it is best to check on the spot.

Foreign residents in the Turkish north can cross to and from the Greek side fairly straightforwardly, but foreign visitors in the north are not permitted by the Greek Cypriot authorities to enter the Greek sector, since they are said to have entered Cyprus through an 'illegal port of entry'. In theory, anyone entering Turkish Cyprus via Ercan airport or the ports of Famagusta or Kyrenia is persona non grata in Greek Cyprus. In practice however, if you arrive at Larnaca or Limassol or Paphos with a North Cyprus stamp in your passport, the customs official simply asks you if he can cancel the stamp before he puts in the Greek Cypriot stamp.

## PASSPORTS AND VISAS

British and US passport holders do not need visas for TRNC and a three month stay is permitted to all visitors. If your flight is simply transiting Turkey en route to Ercan and you do not leave the transit lounge, you do not require a visa. If however, you want to leave the airport and visit Istanbul for a few hours or a few days, you will have to buy a visa, currently £5, as you go out through passport control. These regulations were introduced in November 1989, and the visa must be bought in foreign cash, preferably sterling. The procedure is very quick and simple.

**No visas for British or US citizens**

For those who wish to avoid a North Cyprus stamp in their passports, there is a special form which can be requested from the cabin crew before landing, and this can then be stamped in place of the passport. Contrary to what most people believe, a TRNC stamp in your passport does not in fact prevent a future visit to Greece or her islands. The TRNC stamp is simply cancelled with your permission on arrival in Greece.

# Kyrenia Villa Contacts

*Direct booking with owner for independent holidaymakers*
*fine Villas Cosy Cottages Nice Apartments*
**Total flexibility & choice for up to 10 persons S/C**
**Also, in North Cyprus, sea-side hotels or B & B**
**Prices range from budget to luxury**
**£70 - £700 per week**
*Contact:- Rose or Dennis Fogerty St. Albans*

*Tel & Fax 01727 863853 (24 hrs inc. week-ends)*

# HEALTH

**Healthy climate**

Tap water is safe to drink throughout Turkish Cyprus but does not taste very nice, so most people prefer bottled mineral water which is cheap and widely available. No vaccinations are required or advised. Life expectancy is high at 71, a reflection of the healthy climate and diet. All visitors are entitled to free emergency medical treatment at state hospitals, and all blood banks have been AIDS screened. Chemist shops (Turkish *eczane*) are also well capable of recommending medicines for common holiday illnesses, and many drugs such as antibiotics are available over the counter, with no need for prescriptions.

# TOURIST INFORMATION

In London the North Cyprus Tourist Office is at 28 Cockspur Street, London SW1Y 5BN tel: 0171-930 5069, fax: 0171-839 5282, telex: 8955363, and will send free maps and colour pamphlets, and provide any other help requested.

On the island, there are also tourist offices distributing maps and pamphlets in Kyrenia, Famagusta, Nicosia and Ercan airport.

# TOUR OPERATORS

The following is a list of UK tour operators offering holidays in Turkish Cyprus:

Anatolian Sky, Imex House, 52 Blucher Street, Birmingham B1 1QU; tel: 0121-633 4018; fax: 0121-643 3546.

Blue Moon Travel, 98 George Street, London W1H 5RH; tel: 0171 224 0226, fax: 0171 224 1242.

CTA Holidays Ltd. 41 Pall Mall, London SW1Y 5JG; tel: 0171-930 4853/4/5, fax: 0171-930 1046, telex: 885614.

**The growing list**

Celebrity Holidays & Travel, 18 Frith Street, London W1V 5TS; tel: 0171-734 4386, telex: 269304, fax: 0171-439 2026.

Cricketer Holidays, 4 The White House, Beacon Road, Crowborough, East Sussex, TN8 1AB; tel: 01892 664242, telex: 957392, fax: 01892 662355.

Cyprus Paradise, 689 High Road, London N12 0DA; tel: 0181-343 8888; fax: 0181-343 8800.

European Travel, Unit One, Elephant & Castle Shopping Centre, London SE1 6TE; tel: 0171-277 1458, fax: 0171-701 0034.

Metak Holidays, 69 Welbeck Street, London W1M 7HA; tel: 0171-935 6961, telex: 263188, fax: 0171-224 3675.

Mosaic Holidays, Patman House, George Street, South Woodford, London E18 2LS; tel: 0181-532 9050, fax: 0181-532 9055.

Onur Air, (T K Air Travel and Akdeniz Air), 46 Newington Green, London N16 9PX; tel: 0171-359 9214, fax: 0171-226 3247.

President Holidays Ltd, 542 Kingsland Road, London E8 4AH; tel: 0171-249 4002, fax: 0171-923 1856, telex: 883613.

Regent Holidays (UK) Ltd. Regent House, Regent Street, Shanklin, Isle of Wight, PO37 7AE; tel: 01983 864212/864225, fax: 01983 864197, telex: 86197.

S T Travel & Suntan Holidays, 5 Crossways Parade, Perth Road, London N22 5QX; tel: 0181-888 9118, fax: 0181-888 1534.

Sunquest, 9 Grand Parade, Green Lanes, London N4 1JX; tel: 0181-800 5455, fax: 0181-809 6629.

Tapestry Holidays, 286 Chiswick High Road, London
W4 1PA; tel: 0181-742 0077, fax: 0181-742 0144.

Turkey and Beyond, 29 Marylebone Road, London
NW1 5JX; tel: 0171-486 3338, fax: 0171-486 3339.

Wondersun Holidays, 52 Green Lanes, London N16
9NH; tel: 0171-275 0127, fax: 0171-275 0084.

## CURRENCY AND CHANGING MONEY

The currency in TRNC is the Turkish lira, and there
are no currency restrictions on entry or departure. The
exchange rate is better in the country and in Turkey
than it is abroad. Everyone is willing to change
money: your hotel, your car hire firm, shops and
agencies, and this tends to be easier and cheaper than
using banks. The Sun Rent-a-Car offices in Kyrenia
(beside the Grand Rocks Hotel) and Nicosia (near the
roundabout outside the walls where the Kyrenia road
ends — see map on page 132) offer good rates to
allcomers and transactions take just a few seconds. All
exchange bureaux will accept cash and travellers
cheques, and a few (notably Sergeant Mustafa in
Kyrenia) will even take personal cheques when
supported by a cheque card. Credit cards like
VISA/Barclaycard, Access/Mastercard, and Diner's
Club are accepted by larger hotels and a few big
restaurants, but not at petrol stations or most shops. A
notable exception is Tan Supermarket in Kyrenia, a
useful place at which to stock up when cash is low.
Eurocheques are not widely used. Travellers cheques
are the best medium for visitors, along with cash in
the form of pounds sterling, US dollars or German
DM. The rate for cash is slightly better than for
travellers cheques.

**Best rates
on the
island**

## Costs and budgeting

Costs in Turkish Cyprus are rising, but it is still
reasonable to budget £25 per day for two people, to
cover all food, drink, petrol and entry fees. A meal
out for two in a good restaurant with wine will cost c.

£10-12. Bed and breakfast in a three star hotel is c. £35 for a double room, and car hire is c. £12 per day. 10% VAT was introduced in January 1993.

# GETTING AROUND

## Public transport

Public transport in North Cyprus is limited and you are far better advised to hire a car. However, for those who do not want this extra cost, there are buses, but they are infrequent and do not run to a timetable. Dolmuş (shared) taxis run for set fares between the major towns. Private taxis (with yellow TAKSI signs on the roof) are also reasonably priced, charging fixed official tariffs, but do not cruise and can only be found at taxi-stands, which close at night. There are no functioning railways. Sightseeing tours are widely available from numerous tour operators, such as Mosaic Tri-Sun in Kyrenia, and these are perhaps the best option for non-drivers. Your hotel will be able to advise you on the options.

## Travel by car

As in Greek Cyprus, by far the best way for the visitor to travel is self-drive hire car. All you need is a UK driving licence, and vehicles can be picked up and returned at Ercan airport to avoid transfer costs (which amount to c. £14 per person return). The road network is very good and is being regularly improved,

**No queues** with an increasing number of dual carriageways between the main towns. Car hire rates are cheap, traffic is extremely light by European standards (there are only some 21,000 motor vehicles in the Turkish sector), and it is a joy to drive along near empty roads. Traffic still drives on the left, a hangover from British administration, and petrol, 25% cheaper than in the UK, is still sold by the gallon, another quaint anachronism in our metric-dominated world. Front passengers must wear seat belts. Rear seat belts are a rarity.

## Car hire

There is a plethora of car hire agencies in North Cyprus. Oscar, opposite the Dome Hotel in Kyrenia, leads the field; others are Sun, Atlantik and Memo. In summer they can be fully stretched meeting demand and it is best to book in advance. The minimum age for rental is 21 and the only documents required are a valid UK driving licence, national or international. **Red number plates** Third party insurance is compulsory, but fully comprehensive is recommended at just a few extra pounds a day. Insurance is invalid if you are found to be drunk at the time of an accident. All hire cars have red registration plates and are prefixed by 'Z', so have the advantage of being immediately recognisable by police and military, should you go astray.

Speed limit signs are in miles, while distance markers are in a random mixture of miles and kilometres, which is why both are given throughout this book. The hire cars, too, are a mixture of right-hand and left-hand drive, and if you have a preference, it is best to state it at the time of booking. Traffic drives on the left, so LHD cars are sometimes cheaper. The cheapest cars to hire are usually the Renault 12, at c. £12 per day (inclusive of unlimited mileage and Collision Damage Waiver insurance) while a 4WD Suzuki Jeep costs c. £18. Rates increase in the peak season of July, August and September.

Petrol is cheaper than in Europe, and there is just one grade, 'super'. Unleaded petrol has yet to make its mark. Petrol stations are generally only found in towns, and often shut after 7pm and on Sundays, so it is worth keeping your tank fairly full. The coastline east of Kyrenia, towards the Karpas, is especially sparse in petrol stations, so fill up before setting off on that route.

## Maps

The map provided free by the tourist offices is adequate, but a better one, prepared by Oxford Cartographers in 1989, can now be bought from Rüstem's bookshop near the Saray Hotel in Nicosia (see map on page 132).

## WHERE TO STAY

All rooms have private bathroom facilities unless otherwise indicated. 4 star hotels cost £40-50 for a double room with breakfast, 3 star hotels £35-40, 2 star hotels £25-35. Self-catering villas range from £140-250 per week depending on the number of bedrooms and the season.

## Hotels in Kyrenia Town

### 5 star

**Jasmine Court Apartment Hotel.** Opened 1989. 143 studios and suites set in 30 acres of ground on its own private headland, near Kyrenia harbour. Very high standard of self-catering apartment, with fully equipped kitchen and satellite TV. Central facilities include pool, bars, restaurants, shops, launderette, supervised creche and tennis courts. Rocky cove for swimming and snorkelling. Courtesy bus to Kyrenia.

### 4 star

**Girne View.** Recently built luxury apartment hotel 1km north of Kyrenia on the Nicosia road. Designed for the businessman rather than the tourist, with conference facilities, terrace bar, restaurant and shopping arcade. 39 self-catering studios and 1-3 bedroomed apartments.

**Dome Hotel.** Kyrenia's most famous and long-standing hotel, still favoured by visiting dignitaries. Set on the Kyrenia seafront with its own rocky promontory for sunbathing and ladders down into the sea. 170 large rooms with TV and mini-bar. Balconies overlooking sea or mountains. When deciding, remember that in all these hotels on the north coast, the sea rooms face north, so if for instance you want a sunny breakfast on your balcony, choose the south-facing mountain view. Busy cosmopolitan bar and restaurant with international cuisine. Casino where all currencies are accepted, with roulette, blackjack and backgammon. Boating and fishing trips can be arranged.

The
famous
Dome

### 3 star

**Grand Rocks Hotel.** Formerly the Hesperides, now newly refurbished, in Kyrenia close to the sea. 50 rooms with TV and balcony. Large seawater pool. Beach bar and rocky bathing. Terrace restaurant. Disco.

**Liman Hotel.** On the seafront close to the old harbour. A little noisy by Kyrenia standards. Casino. Attractive café/restaurant under shady trees.

**Ship Inn.** Tudor-style pub with good rooms, large pool, tennis courts and beer garden. One mile west of Kyrenia centre. Good restaurant.

**Dorana Hotel.** In Kyrenia centre, 30 air-conditioned rooms. 300m from the sea. Local cuisine. Well-designed, friendly and family run.

**Family-run hotels**

**Club Kyrenia (Oscar Hotel).** Opened 1987, near the new Kyrenia harbour on a rocky beach. 53 air-conditioned rooms with balcony and sea view. Large pool. Good restaurant. Courtesy bus to town centre 2km away.

### 2 star

**Pia Bella Hotel.** New hotel in Kyrenia centre with air-conditioning, outdoor pool and sun terrace. Comfortable rooms.

**British (formerly Ergenekon) Hotel.** 16 rooms with balcony and good views to old harbour and Kyrenia castle. B&B only. Good simple base.

**King's House.** Simple rooms right on the harbour front, B&B only.

**Anadol Hotel.** 22 rooms in town centre. Indoor and outdoor restaurant. Children's playground.

**Atlantis.** Set back from old harbour but with all balconies overlooking it. 14 air-conditioned rooms. B&B only.

**Socrates Hotel.** 16 rooms with balcony in town centre. Shady courtyard where meals and drinks are served.

### 1 star
**Antique Hotel.** 26 rooms with bath or shower (shared toilet) near the old harbour. Souvenir shop on ground floor. Indoor and outdoor restaurant.

**Bristol Hotel.** Old B&B hotel on main street. 12 rooms with bath or shower (shared toilet). Shady patio at rear.

### Pension
**Set Pansiyon** Part of the Set Pizza restaurant behind the mosque in the old town. 10 simple rooms with shared facilities. No breakfast, but self-serve from kitchen.

## Hotels west from Kyrenia
### 5 star
**Celebrity Hotel.** Modern hotel on private sandy beach 14km (9 miles) west of Kyrenia. 40 air-conditioned double rooms with balcony. Baby sitting service. Disco. Sea view restaurant. Beach bar on the small sandy bay. Watersports, tennis and a sauna. Also 35 attractive and well-equipped self-catering bungalows in a separate complex set round gardens and a pool on the opposite side of the road. Courtesy bus to Kyrenia town centre.

### 4 star
**Luxury caravanserai**

**Château Lambousa.** Opened 1990. Luxury air-conditioned hotel built in traditional caravanserai style, near Lapta 14km (9 miles) west of Kyrenia. Has use of all the facilities of the adjoining Celebrity complex. Set in extensive gardens, with pool and private beach. Courtesy bus.

### 3 star
**Mare Monte Hotel.** Modern hotel on two private coves, mixture of sand and rocks. The main hotel is rather dull, but the separate bungalows are well-

situated right down on the beach. Fragrant gardens. Shady open-air main restaurant from which steps lead down to the sea. Beach bar. Watersports and tennis. 11km (6.5 miles) west of Kyrenia.

**Popular Deniz Kızı**

**Deniz Kızı Hotel.** Popular family run hotel. Set above its own very safe sandy bay, floodlit at night. Wide range of watersports including parascending. Beach café/bar. 55 air-conditioned rooms with balcony, sea or mountain view. Good restaurant with local and international cuisine. Children's playground. 9km (5.5 miles) west of Kyrenia.

**Espri Hotel.** 1 and 2 bed self-catering apartments, all with balconies overlooking the large central pool. Children's pool and play area. 9km (5 miles) west of Kyrenia close to the Deniz Kızı, in its own gardens. 10 minute walk to the beach.

### 2 star

**Golden Bay Hotel.** 10km (6 miles) west of Kyrenia. 25 air-conditioned rooms with balcony. Set above sandy beach, with good terrace restaurant serving local food.

**LA Hotel.** 14km (9 miles) west of Kyrenia. High quality rooms set round a large pool. Satellite TV, minibar, air-conditioning. Private sandy beach connected to the main complex by an underground passage. Tennis court, sauna, gardens. Restaurant and beach bar.

**Soli Inn.** A surprising place to find in this part of the island, 1.5km east of Soli. Once an old camel inn, now a family-run complex opened in 1990. Large pool and children's pool. 13 spacious rooms. Traditional cuisine restaurant and bar.

### B&B/self-catering

**Delightful setting**

**Riverside Villas.** Prettily set on a hillside near Alsancak surrounded by orange and lemon trees. Mixture of 1, 2 or 3 bed villas well-equipped with cooker, fridge/freezer. TV and phone. Tennis court. Large pool, simple bar/restaurant. B&B or HB. Free transport to beach or Kyrenia. Family run.

**The Villa Club.** 8km (5 miles) west of Kyrenia in Alsancak set in 10 acres of orange and lemon groves. Family run. Studios or 1 bed self-catering villas set round a pool. Bar with snacks. 6 minute walk to the beach.

**King's Court**. 12 self-catering apartments, well-furnished and attractive. Opposite the Deniz Kızı. No pool.

**Top Set Hotel**. B&B complex of 24 rooms in two stories set round a central pool. On the sea at Karaoğlanoğlu, 8km (5 miles) west of Kyrenia.

**Club Lapethos**. 26 unit holiday village offering self-catering 1 or 2 bed apartments giving on to garden or pool. Opened 1990. Underground tunnel leads to a private beach. Unusual aquamarine restaurant under pool. 14km (9 miles) west of Kyrenia.

**Karmi Villas**. A range of 2 and 3 bedroomed villas in the village of Karaman (Karmi) are available for rent through travel operators like Regent Holidays, President Holidays and Mosaic (see *Tour Operators* page 17 for addresses).

**Riviera Mocamp.** 5km (3 miles) west of Kyrenia on its private beach. 12 simple self-catering rooms with showers. Bar and restaurant. Camping area.

# Hotels east from Kyrenia
## 3 star
**Ambelia Village.** Set in the mountains near Bellapais, 5km (3 miles) from Kyrenia, an attractive self-catering holiday village covered in mature trees and flowering shrubs, with fine views. Built in traditional style in 1972 by a British company, the complex is now under Turkish management, and much renovation was

completed in 1991. Central restaurant and bar set round small pool. 18 studio flats, steep and longish walk from car park. Several of the 32 privately owned villas (3 bedroomed) are also available for rent. Daily maid service.

**The Olive Tree**. Considered the most luxurious holiday village on the island, owned by Noble Hotels (Asil Nadir's family). Huge pool with excellent sports and entertainment facilities including satellite TV and in-house video. Located just outside Çatalkoy, 5km east of Kyrenia.

**Best beach**

**Club Acapulco**. 10km (6 miles) east of Kyrenia, Club Acapulco is a bungalow complex offering one of the cleanest and best-maintained sandy beaches in North Cyprus. 60 simply furnished chalet rooms. Restaurant and self-service beach cafeteria. Children's playground. Tennis court. Windsurfing. Turkish bath. Jacuzzi. Pool heated and covered in winter.

### Self-catering

**Club Tropicana**. 3km east of Kyrenia, a 10 minute walk to Ozanköy. 12 self-catering villa bungalows, 1 or 2 bed, set round a pool with restaurant and bar serving meals and snacks all day. Family run.

**Hilarion Village**. 18 1 or 2 bed self-catering villa bungalows set on a hillside just below Karmi overlooking the coast. 20 minute walk to the beach. Large pool. Restaurant.

**Altınkaya Bungalows**. 12 1 bed self-catering bungalows round a pool, with restaurant. 5 minute drive from Kyrenia town centre. Pool and restaurant. Family run.

**Bellapais Gardens**. 10 1 bed self-catering villa bungalows next to the abbey with lovely views down the valley to the coast. Pool and restaurant. Hillside setting with gardens.

**Onar Village.** 18 1 bed self-catering villas, and a small hotel, overlooking Kyrenia. Set round the pool, with bar and snacks. Family run. 5 minute drive to Kyrenia.

**Karakum Motel.** On beach 4km (2.5 miles) east of Kyrenia. 8 simple rooms with hot and cold water. Restaurant, bar and camping area.

## Hotels in Nicosia
### 3 star
**Saray Hotel.** Rather faceless hotel in town centre, but Nicosia's best, and well-placed for the old city. 72 rooms. Rooftop bar and restaurant (on 8th floor) with average food, but excellent views.

**Hotel with a view**

### 2 star
**Picnic Hotel.** 10 rooms in a suburb just off the Kyrenia road. Good restaurant. Snacks in shady garden. Disco.

**Sabri's Orient Hotel.** 32 rooms outside the walls on the main Kyrenia road. Restaurant and casino.

### Pensions
**Marmara Pansiyon.** The upstairs of the Chapter House behind the St Sophia Cathedral/Selimiye mosque. Simple and basic, but fun location. Shared facilities.

**Sönmez Pansiyon.** In an attractive old building behind the St Sophia Cathedral, opposite the Lapidary Museum. Simple and basic. Shared facilities.

## Hotels in Famagusta
### 5 star
**Palm Beach Hotel.** The only hotel still accessible on the top edge of Varosha, close to old Famagusta, now the most sophisticated hotel in northern Cyprus. Newly refurbished to luxury standards and under British management. 100 air-conditioned rooms with satellite TV and balcony. Set directly on its own safe sandy beach. Watersports, floodlit tennis courts and

pool. Excellent but expensive restaurant. Nightclub and casino. Boutiques, shops, gym, sauna, Turkish bath and hairdresser.

### 4 star

**Salamis Bay Hotel.** Huge modern complex of 369 air-conditioned rooms with balcony in a rather ugly 'costa del' style, but well located on its own private sandy stretch of bay 11km (6.5 miles) north of Famagusta, a 45 minute walk along the beach to the ruins of Salamis. Olympic size pool and children's pool. Self-contained, with several restaurants, bars, shops. Disco. Tennis courts. Watersports. Children's play area. Additional to the hotel, there are 61 self-catering bungalows and 28 4-bedroomed flats.

**Beautiful design**

**Cyprus Gardens Resort Village.** Opened 1990. Situated 16km (11 miles) east of Famagusta. Attractive Mediterranean style complex of villas or duplex bungalows set in extensive gardens with its own long sandy beach. Watersports, tennis, large pool, children's playground, mini-market, indoor and outdoor restaurants. Horse-riding. Creche.

### 3 star

**Mimoza Hotel.** On the beach close to the Salamis Bay Hotel and with free use of all its facilities. 51 rooms with balcony and sea view. Friendly atmosphere, with open-air restaurant under a mimosa tree by the sea.

**Park Hotel.** Germanic Bavarian style hotel set on the beach 10km (6 miles) north of Famagusta; 20 minutes' walk from the Salamis ruins. 93 rather small rooms, and a little run-down. Watersports, large pool, tennis courts. Excellent but pricey restaurant. Beach bar.

**Rebecca Hotel.** The closest of the hotels to the ruins of Salamis, 9km (5.5 miles) from Famagusta. 42 rooms. 5 minutes' walk to the beach. Large pool. Outdoor café and good restaurant.

**Boğaz Hotel.** 25km (16 miles) from Famagusta on the

northern stretch of the bay, this pleasant hotel makes a good base for the Karpas as well as the Famagusta area. 40 spacious air-conditioned rooms with large balconies. Attractive outdoor terrace shaded by jacaranda trees. The beach has umbrellas and sunbeds, and is reached by crossing the road. Boğaz itself is a small fishing village with several restaurants, if you want to vary the setting for meals. The drive from Boğaz to Kyrenia takes two hours.

**Peaceful setting**

**Sea View**. Opened 1990. 30 air-conditioned rooms set on a hillside above Boğaz village. All rooms with sea view and balconies. Pleasant sun-bathing patio, pool, tennis court, restaurant, 5 minutes' walk to the beach.

## 2 star

**Giranel Hotel.** Small basic family hotel 14 km (9 miles) from Famagusta. 20 rooms. Beach with umbrellas and sun-beds across the road.

## 1 star

**Panorama Hotel.** In new Famagusta 400m from the walled town. 15 rooms, simple but clean. Shared facilities.

**Altun Tabya.** Small simple hotel inside the walls of old Famagusta.

# Hotels in the Karpas

**Karpas Village.** Due to open in 1991, but victim of economic difficulties. Planned as a high standard holiday village built in traditional design on a sandy beach in extensive grounds near Bafra, some 14km (9 miles) north of Boğaz. Air-conditioned rooms with balcony. 6 bars and restaurants, disco, fitness and beauty parlour. Range of water sports, plus riding school and squash courts.

**Open or not?**

**Florya.** 10 simple rooms in a separate annexe to the Florya Restaurant, set on the road some 10km (6 miles) north of Yeni Erenköy, en route to Dipkarpaz.

**Blue Sea Hotel.** Opened 1989, 6 clean well-furnished rooms set in an attractive spot above a beach 10km (6 miles) east of Dipkarpaz en route to the Apostolos Andreas Monastery. Simple restaurant with freshly caught fish. No electricity, but oil lamps provided in the rooms.

## FOOD AND DRINK

The range of food and restaurants on offer in North Cyprus, especially in and around Kyrenia, is enormous, from local cuisine to Chinese, Italian and French. You can snack on a *döner kebab* from a street stall or savour dinner at the chic Abbey House Restaurant in Bellapais, which can hold its own with top restaurants in Europe. Most local specialities will be familiar to visitors to Turkey — various *meze* (selection of hot and cold appetizers), *börek* (hot pastries stuffed with spinach, cheese or meat), kebab, *köfte* (spiced meatballs) *dolma* (stuffed vine leaves), and salads which feature aubergine, tomatoes, onion, cucumber, peppers, watercress, parsley, radishes and olives. Freshly caught fish are widely offered, and include red and grey mullet, lobster, crab, mussels, rock bream, squid and sea bass. Fish is usually simply cooked, grilled or fried, though a few more sophisticated places offer it prepared in special sauces. Specifically Cypriot is the halloumi cheese, with that wonderful rubbery texture, often served grilled as a *meze*. There is also the crumbly white goat's cheese, and thick creamy yogurt (excellent on meat, mixed with herbs, or as a sweet with local mountain honey stirred in). Good quality fresh fruit according to season includes melon, cherries, apples, strawberries, bananas, figs, grapes, oranges, grapefruit and pears. Turkish Delight is available in a variety of flavours, and that with walnuts or pistachios inside is especially delicious.

To wash it all down, there is the cheap and widely available mineral water and the usual range of fizzy drinks, while on the alcoholic front the Turkish Efes beer is very good, as are several of the wines. The

**Choose Turkish wine**

North Cyprus wines (Aphrodite, Kantara and Monarch) are, by their own admission, inferior to those from the Turkish mainland, as wine-making is still a newly developing skill in the north. Of the Turkish wines, those that are consistently the best are those by Kavaklidere and by Doluca. Kavaklidere produce the red Yakut, the white Çankaya, the rosé Lâl, and the primeur Nevşehir. Doluca produce the red and white Doluca and the red Villa Doluca. Also recommended is the Special Reserve Karmen, and the semi-sweet Valdı. Rakı, sometimes known as lion's milk, is the local spirit, clear and aniseed flavoured, drunk either neat with ice or mixed with water, when it turns cloudy. It goes well with *meze*, fish and lamb. The Turkish Yeni Rakı is better than the local Haş Rakı, for the same reasons as the wine. Turkish coffee is widely drunk, introduced here, as elsewhere in the eastern Mediterranean, by the Ottomans in the 15th century. It is drunk *sade* (without sugar), *orta* (medium sugar), or *şekerli* (heavily sugared).

## WHERE TO EAT

As on the Turkish mainland, restaurant hours are very flexible and there is generally no problem about eating lunch at 4pm and dinner at 10pm if that is what happens to suit you. Turkish Cypriots eat out a lot themselves, especially at weekends, and the whole family partakes, from grandparents to babies.

### Restaurants in Kyrenia town

The selection on offer is huge and those mentioned here are only by way of introduction. **Çanlı Balik** and the **Set Fish** restaurants are generally considered the best for fish on the old harbour front, on the raised-up section near the centre. Also on the harbour front, the **Maribou** offers a few more interestingly prepared fish dishes, and takes credit cards. The **Harbour Club**, a few steps away towards the castle, is a popular place in the evenings for a more expensive meal, with a large menu of French-style dishes. 'Downstairs' has good Turkish *meze*. **Le Château** offers exclusive

**Harbour setting**

French cuisine.

A little behind the old harbour is another cluster of places, generally better value, though you do, of course, sacrifice the view. Especially fine is the **Set Pizza**, beside the old mosque, situated in an exquisite Italianate split-level courtyard. Service is attentive and the pizzas are good. Further along the same street is **The Cosy Corner** with a pleasant atmosphere. Behind the mosque, up a flight of steps, is **The Club**, a beautiful old white Greek house with an arcaded verandah. It is open evenings only and has a bar and restaurant. The food is nothing special, but the ambience is unusual. Upstairs is the local football club's headquarters. Near the covered market is **Nostalgia** with a pub-like atmosphere, good for a *meze* lunch. **Efendi's House** in the Turkish quarter near the main Post Office offers top French cuisine from 7.30pm in an old Ottoman house with lovely gardens.

Among restaurants favoured by expatriates are **The Chinese House**, (former Dragon House), the **Hong Kong Chinese** restaurant in the Halkevi behind the castle, **Grapevine** and **Papillon**. **Tepebaşı**, set well inland with a terrace overlooking the town, is probably the best Turkish Cypriot restaurant offering local specialities at very reasonable prices.

## Restaurants west of Kyrenia

**Dingo's Inn** is at Boğazköy on the way to Nicosia, 6km (3.5 miles) from Kyrenia, just after crossing the mountain chain. Turn left to Boğaz and Dikmen and the restaurant is on the right after c.400m. Turkish Cypriot cuisine at reasonable prices. Spacious indoor and outdoor eating. Playground and small children's zoo.

The coast west from Kyrenia till Lapta is the most developed stretch of coastline in North Cyprus, and there are numerous hotels and restaurants. The **Veranda** restaurant and beach bar at Karaoğlanoğlu offers international cuisine. On the sea beside the Silver Waves Hotel at Karaoğlanoğlu is the **Artemis International Restaurant**, offering good food in opulent, tasteful surroundings with local antiques as decor and a new sea terrace for summer dining. Also at Karaoğlanoğlu is **Yama Restaurant**, excellent for *meze* and fish; **The Orchard**, offering local cuisine, and **Kyrenia Star**, with good international and local cuisine. **Altınkaya**, set overlooking the sea near Invasion Beach, just before the Deniz Kızı Hotel, 8km (5 miles) west of Kyrenia, is reckoned to be the best fish restaurant, offering a set *meze* with your choice of fish. Very popular with Turkish Cypriots. You can eat indoors or outside on the terrace with a sea view. Just beside the Celebrity Hotel is **Rita on the Rocks**, named after the owner, an unusual restaurant and bar set above the sea on a landscaped terrace, with its own pool. **Marmaris Restaurant** is also next to the Celebrity Hotel, on a promontory over the sea. It offers good service and *meze*, and has live music on Friday and Saturday evenings. Just west of Rita on the Rocks is the excellent **Şevket's Bar and Restaurant**, family run with traditional Cypriot cuisine and vegetarian specialities and sporting a swimming pool for the use of customers.

**The best fish**

If you want a change from the sea, there are good restaurants in the mountain village of Karmi (Turkish Karaman), 4km (2.5 miles) inland from Karaoğanoğu. **Kismet View** is a good restaurant/bar featuring Lebanese cuisine, with good views and balconies. The **Duckworth House Restaurant**, open all day from 10am for coffee and afternoon tea as well as lunch and dinner, has pretty gardens and its own pool. European cuisine. The others are the **Treasure**, at the entrance of the village, formerly the Greek school,

**Inland eating**

with a panoramic terrace, **Levant**, by the church, and the **Crow's Nest**, more like a pub, nearer the centre. At Ilgaz, a mountain village west of Karmi, is **Flintstones**, offering simple lunches, popular with expatriates (closed Wednesdays). Also away from the sea is **Old Milos** at Alsancak, a modern building beside an old mill and spring. It has taverna music three times a week. The **Saint Tropez** at Alsancak is an exclusive French restaurant. Beşpinar, at the highest point above Lapta, has a fine setting.

West of Lapta, eating places are few and far between, though there is a pleasant cluster of beach restaurants near Yedidalga, between Soli and Vouni, offering simple fare of *meze*, kebabs and fish, with willing service.

## Restaurants east of Kyrenia

Near Karakum, some 2km east of Kyrenia, watch out for the sign to the right to the **Courtyard Inn**. Run by two British couples, it is set in lovely gardens, with indoor and outdoor eating. The food is excellent and varied and the atmosphere relaxed. Adopted by Cricketer Holidays, its handful of rooms is almost always full. On the Çatalköy road 5km east of Kyrenia, **Paradise Restaurant** is open 10am to midnight and has a 20m pool.

A little way beyond the Bellapais junction the **Mountain House** offers good Turkish *meze* and mixed European cuisine (closed Sundays).

Bellapais village in the hills above Kyrenia boasts several restaurants.

In front of the abbey is the well-known **Tree of Idleness**, and inside the abbey itself, set in what were the abbey kitchens, it the **Kybele Restaurant**, with the best views of all.

The village of Ozanköy, below Bellapais, also has a few attractive restaurants, notably **The Old Mill**, **The Five Fingers** and **Happy Garden**, all offering Turkish Cypriot cuisine. Çatalköy, the village just inland from the coast road, some 3km east of Kyrenia, has the popular fish restaurant of **Zia's**.

The road along the northern coast towards the

Karpas is currently sparsely provided with restaurants. The first you come to is at the **Club Acapulco** holiday village, with its self-service restaurant (hot and cold food) on the beach, some 10km (6 miles) east of Kyrenia. 2km further east is **Lara Beach**, a pretty bay

**Simple fare**

with a simple but attractive restaurant and picnic area. After this, there is nothing until Alakati, 18km (12 miles) from Kyrenia, where the two simple kebab restaurants of **St Kathleen's** and **Hoca's** are together on either side of the main road. St Kathleen's is named after the early ruined basilica on the flat ground between it and the sea.

Making a 2km detour inland at Esentepe, there is a simple kebab restaurant opposite the old church. Otherwise there is nothing along the coast until Kantara, where again you must go inland and climb up to the village of Kantara to find a restaurant in the square, some 5km (3 miles) before the castle.

## Restaurants in Nicosia

There are no outstanding restaurants in Nicosia, and eating in the capital falls into the category of a necessity rather than a delight. Names to look out for are **Anibal**, the oldest kebab restaurant, **Amasyalı**, in the centre with tasty fast food, the **Continental**, behind the Saray Hotel, with good kebabs, the rooftop **Saray Hotel** restaurant, with middling food but the best views.

## Restaurants in Famagusta region

There are a couple of interesting places to eat in Famagusta, both near Varosha. **La Cheminée** is a French restaurant in an unlikely setting by itself, near the barbed wire fence of Varosha, not far from the Palm Beach Hotel. Excellent and varied food with an

**Unusual décor**

extensive wine list. The **Cyprus House** is in the old police station on former Independence Avenue, near the old court house. Unusual paintings and antiques for décor, with good *meze* and other Cypriot dishes. Occasional belly dancer in the evenings.

In and around the old walls of Famagusta there is nowhere special, just a variety of simple kebab houses and cafés. The tea garden behind the cathedral/mosque has a pleasant setting, and the **Petek Pastahanesi** near the Sea Gate is wonderful for sticky pastries and ice cream.

At Salamis there is quite a good restaurant just outside the sea entrance to the site, and at Boğaz at the northern end of Famagusta Bay there are several pleasant fish restaurants on the water's edge. **Mr Li's** at Long Beach is a Chinese restaurant on the beach front at Long Beach Country Club 2km beyond the Salamis Bay Hotel.

## Restaurants in the Karpas

The Karpas, the remotest and least developed part of North Cyprus, is only sparsely provided with restaurants. Polly Peck's Karpaz Holiday Village near Bafra was unfortunately not completed before Asil Nadir's bankruptcy.

3km northeast of Yeni Erenköy on the Dipkarpaz road is the **Karpaz Plaj** restaurant, a simple clean place offering fish and kebabs on a good sandy beach. 10km (6 miles) northeast of Yeni Erenköy on the same road is the same road is the **Florya** restaurant, with simple kebabs and *köfte*. There is no real beach but it is possible to swim from the rocky bay below.

10km (6 miles) east of Dipkarpaz on the Apostolos Andreas Monastery road is the modest **Blue Sea Hotel and Restaurant** opened in summer 1989, serving freshly caught fish. Very attractive setting above a beach and little harbour. Willing service.

## Tipping

Tipping is not expected when a service charge is added to the bill, though a small extra amount will indicate gratitude for especially attentive service. Tipping is also not usual for taxis.

## CLIMATE

Spring and autumn are the best times to visit. From late February until late April the island is alive with colourful flowers, and in March and April the citrus trees are in blossom. From 1st June until mid-September it never rains, and July and August are the hottest months.

**Ideal in spring and autumn**

The rainy season is meant to be from November until February, although you do get occasional rainy days in October and even more so in March. December and January are the wettest months, while January and February are the coldest months. Rainstorms do occur in April and May, but these never last more than a day or two before brilliant sunshine breaks out again.

## Average temperatures in °C

| Jan | Feb | Mar | Apr | May | Jun | Jul | Aug | Sep | Oct | Nov | Dec |
|-----|-----|-----|-----|-----|-----|-----|-----|-----|-----|-----|-----|
| 14 | 14 | 15 | 18 | 21 | 24 | 29 | 29 | 25 | 23 | 18 | 13 |

## Average maximum temperatures in °C

| Jan | Feb | Mar | Apr | May | Jun | Jul | Aug | Sep | Oct | Nov | Dec |
|-----|-----|-----|-----|-----|-----|-----|-----|-----|-----|-----|-----|
| 18 | 19 | 21 | 23 | 27 | 30 | 36 | 36 | 32 | 28 | 24 | 17 |

## Average sea temperatures in °C

| Jan | Feb | Mar | Apr | May | Jun | Jul | Aug | Sep | Oct | Nov | Dec |
|-----|-----|-----|-----|-----|-----|-----|-----|-----|-----|-----|-----|
| 11 | 12 | 14 | 19 | 21 | 24 | 26 | 27 | 26 | 23 | 14 | 11 |

# CLOTHING

North Cyprus is not a dressy place and comfortable informal clothing is best. Although nominally Muslim, Turkish Cypriots are very relaxed, and you can dress here as you would when holidaying in Italy or Spain.

**Casual dress**

Good comfortable shoes are essential for climbs up to the mountain castles. Bikinis are fine and toplessness is increasing, especially among Germans on the private fee-paying beaches.

From the end of October until mid-April it is usually still chilly, especially in the evenings. Take a light raincoat in the winter months, or an umbrella, as rain storms are very hard.

# BEACHES

The whole of Famagusta Bay is one long sandy beach, and any hotel built along it will have excellent bathing.

**Famagusta has the best**

The northern coast is much more mixed, with sandy bays interspersed with rocky coves, cliffs and headlands. On many beaches, especially the sandy ones, you will notice clumps of eel grass, a kind of seaweed, which accumulates and needs to be removed regularly. Local environmentalists, frequently expatriate residents, are active in beach clear-up days. North Cyprus does not escape the general pollution of the Mediterranean, and tar along with plastic bottles, etc, often mar virgin beaches. Clean sand is the main advantage of using one of the private fee-paying beaches. Prevailing winds are from the west, so a bay tucked into the eastern side of a promontory generally offers wind protection, the calmest water, and the least tar and eel grass. There are no tides at all so all beaches are safe from currents.

*Beach of the Deniz Kızı Hotel*

In Kyrenia itself swimming possibilities are limited to the Dome Hotel, from its rocky promontory (open to non-residents), and the crowded but sandy public beach beside Kyrenia Castle, formerly known as The Slab and restricted to members of the now defunct Country Club. The usual practice therefore, for those based in or around Kyrenia, is to use one of the numerous beaches further along the coast, maybe even trying a different one each time. The following may help you decide.

## Beaches west from Kyrenia

**Riviera Mocamp**, 4km west of Kyrenia, near Karağlanoğlu, signposted from the main road. Small sandy bay for children, but otherwise rocky, with a jetty for swimming and diving. Restaurant and showers.

**Altınkaya Beach**, 8km (5 miles) west, below the restaurant of the same name. You can drive the car right down to the beach, handy if you have lots of gear, by following the sign for Yavaz Çikartma, just west of Attinkaya restaurant from the main road. The SunSet Restaurant and Beach Bar is on the beach at the end of the long sandy bay. The water is shallow and very safe for children with air mattresses and dinghies, as there is an island (known as Golden Rock) just offshore (so close you can wade across to it) protecting the entry to the bay.

**Range of water sports**

**Deniz Kızı**, belonging to the hotel of the same name, but open, like all the hotel beaches, to fee-paying non-residents. 9km (5.5 miles) west of Kyrenia, a sandy bay with safe, sheltered bathing. Bamboo umbrella shades, showers and changing cabins. Beach café and children's play area. Variety of unusual watersports, the best on the island, provided by Dolphin Sailing.

In the next bay west from the Deniz Kızı stands the unfinished hulk of the 5 star Crystal Cove Hotel on its own small beach.

**Mare Monte**, 12km (7.5 miles) west, belonging to the hotel. Longish walk down steps to the beach, a mixture of rock and sand. Floating raft offshore, straw umbrellas, beach café, children's playground. A 10 minute walk west along the beach takes you to the Roman remains of Lambousa.

**Celebrity**, the hotel beach, but very small. 14km (9 miles) west, with all amenities.

**LA Beach**, just beyond the Celebrity complex, with sunbeds, umbrellas and a snack bar.

**Horseshoe Bay**, 20km (12.5 miles) west of Kyrenia and 3km east of Kayalar. A shingle beach with pretty coloured pebbles, good for snorkelling but not suitable for young children. No amenities.

**Towards Korucam Burnu (Cape Kormakiti)**: All along this stretch of wild coastline west from Kayalar are many small sandy and rocky bays backed by cliffs. Attractive and secluded, they are also often difficult to reach, involving a scramble down from the road and a longish walk. The area around the cape itself near the lighthouse used to be military and prohibited, but has recently been demilitarised and is approachable.

## Beaches east from Kyrenia
**Karakum**, a small horseshoe cove of sand ideal for young children, just 2 miles east of Kyrenia. Reached by forking left at the Hong Kong Chinese restaurant, then turning right along a dirt track once it reaches the shore.

**Acapulco**, belonging to the holiday village, Club Acapulco, 10km (6 miles) east of Kyrenia. Probably the best beach on the north coast for children, and one of the most expensive, with a long stretch of clean **Good** sand bounded by rocky promontories. On the eastern **beach** promontory stands the excavated Neolithic site of **restaurant** Vrysi. Shallow water and gentle shelving. Straw umbrellas, sunbeds, watersports. Self-service beach restaurant. Children's playground. Tennis court.

**Lara Beach**, 2km east of Acapulco, a very pretty bay with rock and sand. Sometimes a little 'tarry'. Attractive restaurant with picnic area. Fine for children, but adults may prefer the area of smooth limestone rock slabs and rock pools beyond the western edge of the sandy bay. The cliffs behind these rock slabs are also fun to explore, with caves and other weird formations.

**Alakati**, 18km (12 miles) from Kyrenia, the longest stretch of sand on the north coast, now designated *Halk Plaji* (Public Beach), with all the litter that this entails. You will recognise it both from the sand dunes and from the fact that the whole area is now fenced in, for it was leased by the former Turkish Cypriot multi-millionaire Asil Nadir (of Polly Peck fame) for development. A holiday village was under construction in this, what is unquestionably one of the most beautiful spots on the island, but now its completion date remains uncertain. Inland the view is directly on to the five peaks of Beşparmak Mountain. Access from the main road is possible via a number of dirt tracks, and then there is usually a walk of 200-300m to the sea. It is sometimes called 'Turtle Beach' as a favoured spot for the loggerhead turtles to come and lay their eggs.

**Turtle Beach**

**Karaağaç**, 25.5km (16 miles) from Kyrenia, a small secluded shingly bay not visible from the road. The track off is marked by a small group of stone farm buildings, but is too rocky to be driven far. The walk to the sea takes about 10 minutes, and takes you through the ruins of ancient Kharcha, for which this beach was once the harbour.

**Yalı Gazinosu**, 53km (33 miles) from Kyrenia, a cluster of small sandy beaches visible from the road. With no amenities.

**Kaplıca**, 69km (43 miles) from Kyrenia, a long remarkably clean sandy beach just before the turn-off to Kaplıca and Kantara Castle, whose outline can be seen on the crest of the mountains above. The derelict shell of a large hotel stands in front of it, and redevelopment of this lovely spot will probably not be long in coming. Good picnic spot en route to Kantara.

**Yeni Erenköy**, 67km (42 miles) east, soon after the town a track leads down on to the sandy Halk Plaj or public beach which has a restaurant, showers and cabins that function from April to October.

**Karpaz Plaj**, 2km beyond Yeni Erenköy at the Florya restaurant. Swimming is possible, though a bit tricky, in the rocky bay below. There are three abandoned Greek churches.

**Ayios Philon**, some 4km beyond Dipkarpaz, the sandy bay below the ruined basilica, once the harbour of ancient Karpasia. No amenities.

**Aphendrika**, 10km (6 miles) beyond Dipkarpaz, the end of the road on the northern coastline, where a group of three picturesque ruined churches stand. The walk to the sea is a long one, 1.5km to the east of the ruins across the fields. The beach is sandy with advancing dunes and is utterly deserted.

**Remote beaches**
The southern coastline of the Karpas has many beaches, often sandy, but most are difficult to reach and have no amenities whatsoever. The most magnificent stretch of all lies close to the tip, a few kilometres before the Apostolos Andreas Monastery. It is known as Golden Sands, though the wild dunes often look more red than golden, and is a major breeding ground for sea turtles. It is marred only by tar and accumulated sea debris. The tip itself is rocky and swimming is very tricky.

## FLORA AND FAUNA

**Natural beauty**
North Cyprus offers many unspoilt landscapes with hundreds of wild flowers. The best season for flowers is February to May, when a few of those to be seen are giant yellow fennel, cyclamen, crown anemones,

pink rock roses, purple iris, vetch, orchid, anchusa, gladioli and yellow crowfoot.

The mountain ridges that run from behind Lapta towards St Hilarion castle and from the Five Finger mountain towards Esentepe make excellent walking for botanists and birdwatchers.

**Proposed national park**

The undeveloped Karpas peninsula is particularly rich in flowers and wildlife generally, and is projected to become a national park, both to protect the nesting beaches for the threatened loggerhead turtles and to protect migrating birds from over-hunting.

See page 220 for *Further reading*.

## WALKS

**Maps for walkers**

The National Trust of the TRNC (Turkish Republic of North Cyprus), at PO Box 582, Girne, Mersin 10, Turkey, produces maps for walkers. Maps published so far cover a tour of Kyrenia's old harbour, a long mountain walk between St Hilarion Castle and Lapta, a tour of Famagusta and an uphill trek eastwards from Bellapais towards Buffavento Castle. They are usually available from local hotels or at Kyrenia's Green Jacket Bookshop.

**Free guided walks**

The TRNC Tourism Planning Office has also produced a leaflet on walks called Mountain Trail "A" and has started to offer free guided walks setting off from Karaman on Sundays at 9am, building up to three times a week depending on demand. These walks are organised via Blue Moon Travel Ltd, 98 George Street, London W1H 5RH, tel: 0171-224 0226, fax: 0171-224 1242, a tours and excursions specialist who also have an office in Nicosia.

**Loveliest walks**

In general the Kyrenia mountain range offers the best walking, with many quiet forest tracks well maintained by the Forestry Commission. Some of the loveliest include the walk from Karaman (Karmi) village up to St Hilarion Castle, an easy 3km walk taking one hour; from Malatya to Ilgaz, a 1.5km walk passing a waterfall on the way; from Ilgaz to Karaman, a 4km walk taking one and a half hours; along the ridge from the Five Finger Mountain pass towards the Armenian monastery; and along the ridge from St Hilarion towards Lapta. This track, also drivable in a saloon car, passes a fountain at about 8km, then at 10km reaches Sisklip, the point above Malatya where there is a junction with three tracks. The middle track continues 9.2km past Mt Selvili at 1,023m to reach the tarmac road down to Karşıyaka, while the right fork leads 6.3km to Lapta; the left fork leads down to the tarmac at Akçiçek and is of less interest to walkers. The village of Ozanköy has many lovely walks through ancient olive groves in all directions and specifically up towards Bellapais and its abbey. Lapta is another village particularly well placed for walks into the olive and citrus groves and up into the mountains.

The following hotels are situated in good spots for walks into surrounding unspoilt countryside:

**Good spots to start a walk**

**The Olive Tree**, 4 star, a luxury hotel surrounded by olive groves and citrus trees in the foothills of the Five Finger Mountain.

**Deniz Kızı**, 3 star, on its own sandy bay but with lovely walks inland along country lanes and up tracks into the hills.

**LA Hotel**, 3 star, 9 miles west of Kyrenia, with attractive walks through citrus groves towards the backdrop of mountains and Lapta.

**Ambelia Village**, 3 star. The well-established gardens are most attractive, and if you do not mind the gradients you can walk uphill to join paths into the mountains. The land to the north and west of the complex is a military camp, so all sorties must be south or east.

**Riverside Holiday Village**, 2 star, surrounded by 10 acres of orange and lemon groves and mature gardens, with its own aviary and duckpond. It is located on the outskirts of Alsancak, with some of the island's best and prettiest walking nearby.

**Hilarion Village**, 2 star, set in the mountains 2 miles west of and a little below the ruins of St Hilarion Castle.

**Onar Village**, 2 star, above Kyrenia in ten acres of grounds and with attractive walks into the foothills.

**Bellapais Gardens**, 2 star, with lush vegetation and palm trees round its pool and steep walks leading up through the village on to mountain tracks or down towards Ozanköy.

**Club Tropicana**, 1 star, Ozanköy, well placed for country walks in all directions, and a good base for cycling holidays.

**Good beach walks**

The hotels on Famagusta bay, like the **Park Hotel**, 4 star, and the **Cyprus Gardens**, 3 star, are very well located for long walks/strolls along the sandy beach towards Salamis, though not so much for inland walking, where the scenery tends to be flat and uninteresting.

In addition to these hotels, there are also many villas for rent, especially in the village of Karaman (Karmi), which are well situated for strolls off into the mountains.

## CYCLING

**Ideal for cycling**

North Cyprus with its quiet roads and scant traffic is an ideal place for cycling, and 18-gear bicycles can be hired locally or reserved in advance through companies like the UK's Imperial Tourism, 79 Lewisham High Street, London SE13 5JX, tel: 0181-318 9000, for £2 or £3 sterling a day. Cyprus Gardens Hotel in Famagusta offers Rent-a-Bicycle, and its location makes for easy cycling along the flat land to Salamis and even up towards the Karpas.

The intrepid Mike and Ann Edwards of Havant were kind enough to write in after their cycling holiday on a tandem, brought with them from the UK, and said they found both the northern coast road heading east from Kyrenia and the roads on the Karpas particularly suitable for cycling. They **Avoid the** suggested that the main roads between Kyrenia and **busy** Nicosia and between Famagusta and Nicosia were best **roads** avoided as they were busier, with faster traffic and more lorries. They recommended avoiding the central plain altogether, but found the Five Finger Mountain pass (Kyrenia to Ercan) surprisingly quiet.

## SPORTS

Watersports are the most widely practised and most hotel beaches offer windsurfing, water-skiing and pedaloes. The Deniz Kızı Hotel has a British company called Dolphin Sailing on the premises, which offers tuition in all the usual watersports including dinghy sailing, as well as offering some exciting new ones like parascending and aqua-rocket. Ambelia Holiday Village near Bellapais holds introductory diving lessons in its pool.

North Cyprus offers some of the best diving sites in the Mediterranean, including the underwater formations at Mansinis Reef and the ancient shipwreck at Kyrenia, as well as the opportunity to photograph and feed the wildlife at Fred's Reef. Fish abound, including among their number stingray, amberjack, cuckoo wrasse, scorpionfish, bream and grouper. Tuition for both complete novices and advanced divers is available through Cyprus Diving Centres at their two locations, Kyrenia Diving Centre, 21 Philecia Court, Girne, Kibris, tel: 8156087, and Fred Dive Ltd, 7 Gaz Kemal Aşik Road, Lefkoşa, tel: 8151743.

Besides watersports, there are tennis courts at the Mare Monte Hotel, the Celebrity Hotel, and Club Acapulco in the Kyrenia area, and at the Salamis Bay Hotel, the Palm Beach Hotel, the Cyprus Gardens Hotel and the Park Hotel in the Famagusta area. All are open to non-residents except the Palm Beach and the Park. There are two riding schools, the Four Horseshoes and the Tunaç, both at Karaoğlanoğlu, just east of Kyrenia, and both offer day rides into the mountains with picnics. Riding is also available at the Cyprus Gardens Hotel Village near Famagusta, and at the Mare Monte Hotel, to residents and non-residents. There is a 7-hole practice golf course open to all at Yeşilyurt, west of Güzelyurt.

## ENTERTAINMENT

Evening entertainment is generally restricted to discos and casinos, most of which are to be found in the big hotels like the Dome and the Grand Rocks in Kyrenia, and the Palm Beach and the Salamis Bay in Famagusta. Kyrenia is the best provided and, very occasionally, there are also musical performances held in Kyrenia Castle or at Bellapais Abbey.

For daytime entertainment apart from shopping and sightseeing, you could try the Wildlife Park established in 1985 in 16 hectares of land 10 minutes from Kyrenia, or the Famagusta Municipal Zoo set in public gardens with fountains, tennis courts and a children's amusement area. It has gazelles, monkeys, sheep, squirrels, birds and fish and an entomological museum.

## PUBLIC AND RELIGIOUS HOLIDAYS

| | |
|---|---|
| 1 January | New Year's Day |
| 23 April | National Sovereignty and Children's Day |
| 1 May | Labour Day |
| 19 May | Youth and Sports Day |
| 20 July | Peace and Freedom Day |
| 1 August | TMT Day (birth of Turkish Cypriot Resistance Movement) |
| 30 August | Victory Day |
| 29 October | Turkish National Day |
| 15 November | Independence Day (proclamation of TRNC) |
| 25 December | Christmas Day |

Turkey and North Cyprus follow the Gregorian calendar like the rest of Europe but, being predominantly Muslim, the major Islamic festivals are celebrated. The dates of these religious holidays change each year as they are calculated by the lunar system, and so move forward by about 11 days in the Gregorian calendar each year. There are two major Islamic holidays, the equivalents, if you like, of our Christmas and Easter. The first is Kurban Bayramı, the Feast of the Sacrifice, which commemorates Abraham's willingness to sacrifice his son Isaac. Each family traditionally sacrifices an animal (a sheep or a chicken, according to means), which is then cooked and eaten in large family gatherings. In 1995 Kurban Bayramı fell around mid-May. It is a four day national holiday, the longest of the year. The second festival celebrates the end of fasting during the 30 day month of Ramadan and is called Şeker Bayramı, the Sugar Festival, because much sweet food is eaten. It is a three day national holiday and in 1995 fell in early March. Ramadan itself is not strictly observed as a fasting month, and restaurants stay open as usual during the day.

**Muslim festivals**

## SHOPPING AND SOUVENIRS

The best shopping is to be found in Kyrenia, along the main street and in the side roads off it. Nicosia also has good shops but they are scattered and therefore more difficult for the visitor to find and use. Things to look out for are pottery (the best shop is Dizayn 74 on the way to Karaoğlanoğlu opposite 'The Ship'), ceramics, leather shoes and bags, rugs and kilims, canvas suitcases and bags (very cheap and handy when your new purchases threaten to burst your existing suitcase), basketwork, dolls, jewellery, copper, brass and lacework. Kyrenia also has some good clothes boutiques, including a Benetton. All items are priced in Turkish lira and prices are frequently cheaper than in the UK. Prices tend to be fixed and not subject to haggling.

**Good prices, usually fixed**

Food shopping is generally cheapest in the Belediye Pazarı, the town market, where stalls selling fruit, vegetables, meat, fish and all other household necessities are grouped together under one roof.

Duty free allowances are 200 cigarettes or 250 grams of tobacco, 1 litre of wine, 1 litre of spirits and 0.30cl of perfume.

## WEIGHTS AND MEASURES

North Cyprus is a total jumble of measuring systems, with all sorts of Ottoman relics which are still used, curiously, in the Greek sector as well. The oke, for example, is the standard weight measure, and remember when buying fruit, meat and vegetables that, at 2.8lbs, it is rather more than a kilo, which is only 2.2lbs. There are 400 drams to the oke, and 800 okes = a ton. The other Ottoman measure still in use is the donum, the land measure, which is a little under a third of an acre. The British administration left its heritage of driving on the left, and all the distance signposts which remain from that time are in miles, while more recent ones are generally, though not always, in kilometres. Both are therefore given throughout the book, especially as hire cars may be either right or left hand drive and are calibrated in kilometres or miles accordingly.

**British leftovers**

## POST

Postal rates are very reasonable with one rate for Europe and the Middle East. Postcards take about 10-14 days to reach most European destinations, letters 5-7 days. Post boxes are yellow and are found in the main streets of all towns and villages. When sending items to North Cyprus, the code 'Mersin 10, Turkey' should always appear, rather than 'North Cyprus', otherwise they may be misdirected to Greek Cyprus.

## OPENING HOURS

Shops are generally open from 8am-1pm and 2-5.30pm in winter, while in summer the hours shift to 7.30am-1pm and 4-6pm. Most shops shut on Sundays, though a few grocery stores remain open. If you are desperate to buy snack food after 6pm it is useful to know about the little kiosk near the traffic lights in Kyrenia, selling nuts, dried fruits and sweets, as well as beer and other alcohol, and which stays open till 9pm. There is a daily fruit and vegetable market near this kiosk behind the bus station, which stays open till around 4 or 5pm. Banks are open from 8.30am-12noon; money changing offices are open all day.

## TIME

From the end of March until mid-September, North Cyprus is on GMT +3; in winter GMT +2. The usual time difference with the UK is therefore two hours.

## TELEPHONE, FAX AND TELEX

To telephone North Cyprus from the UK, dial 010 (international), then 90 (Turkey country code), then 392 (North Cyprus code), before dialling the relevant town code, and finally the actual number itself. Kyrenia is 815, Nicosia is 227 or 228, and Famagusta is 366. To dial the UK from North Cyprus it is 010 (international), then 44 (UK country code), then the town code minus the initial 0, then the number itself.

**Modern facilities**
It is not possible to make calls from the Turkish sector to the Greek sector of Cyprus. Modern fax and telex facilities are widely available throughout the country.

## ELECTRICITY

220-240 volts AC, with 2-pin continental plugs and occasionally UK 3 pin plugs. Bring a travel plug to cover all options.

## MUSEUMS AND MONUMENTS

Entry to museums and ancient monuments usually costs TL1000. Most museums are closed weekends, while ancient monuments and sites tend to be open daily. Individual opening hours are given in the site descriptions.

## MEDIA

The *Cyprus Times* is a new weekly paper in English, giving a round-up of news and events in North Cyprus. Turkish Cypriot TV and Turkish TV channels are received. There is news in English, plus a few imported English programmes, usually soaps.

BBC World Service main frequencies are 17.64MHz and 15.07MHz. The British Forces Broadcasting Service in the Sovereign Bases in Greek Cyprus can be heard clearly in the Famagusta area on 99.6MHz and 95.3MHz, and in the Nicosia area on 89.7MHz and 91.9MHz.

## FOREIGN MISSIONS AND ASSOCIATIONS

Turkey is the only country to have a full embassy in North Cyprus. Britain, the USA, Germany and Australia have liaison offices in Turkish Nicosia for consular services and for cultural and social relations with TRNC.

**British High Commission**: 23 Mehmet Akif Avenue, Nicosia, tel: 227 1938. Open 7.30am-1pm Mon to Fri. This office can also relay any calls through to the High Commission in the Greek sector. The British Council shares the same premises and offers a library, open 7.30am-1.30pm and 3.30-6.30pm Mon to Fri, closed Wed afternoons. From its offices in Greek Nicosia the British Council organises some cultural events in North Cyprus, like films and exhibitions.

**Liaison offices**
The All-Party British Parliamentary Group of the 'Friends of Turkish Cyprus', established at the House of Commons, London, in 1985, promotes the Turkish Cypriot viewpoint and aims to help find a solution to the Cyprus problem that treats both communities fairly.

**The American Centre**: open 8.00am-5.00pm Mon to Fri. 20 Güner Türkmen St, Nicosia, tel: 227 2443.

**German Cultural Centre**: 28 Kasım St, Nicosia, tel: 227 5161.

**Australian High Commission**: open Tues and Thurs only, 9.00am-12.30pm. Saray Hotel, Nicosia, tel: 227 7332.

**Association Culturelle Chypriote Turque Française**, established in 1985, is based in Turkish Nicosia to help promote cultural relations with France.

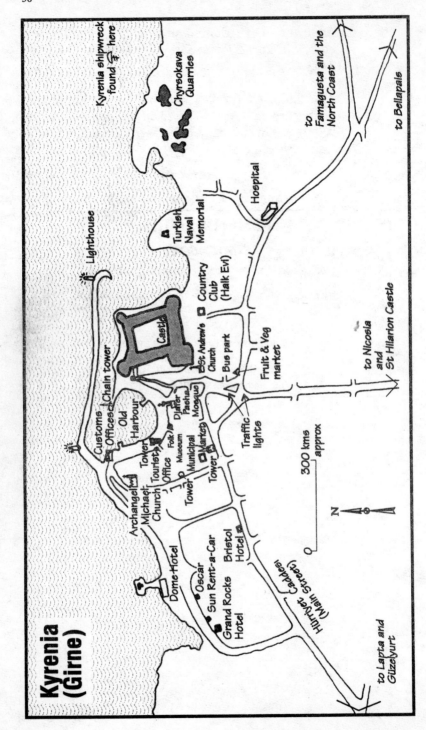

# Kyrenia (Girne)

Kyrenia shipwreck found here

Chyrsokava Quarries

Lighthouse

Turkish Naval Memorial

Hospital

to Famagusta and the North Coast

to Bellapais

Castle

Country Club (Halk Evi)

Customs Officess Chain tower

Old Harbour

St Andrews Church

Bus park

Fruit & Veg market

Djafer Pasha Mosque

Archangel Michael Church

Tower

Tourist Office

Museum

Folk

Municipal Market

Tower

Traffic lights

to Nicosia and St Hilarion Castle

300 kms approx

N

Dome Hotel

Oscar

Sun Rent-a-Car

Grand Rocks Hotel

Bristol Hotel

Hürriyet Caddesi (Main Street)

to Lapta and Güzelyurt

Chapter Three

# Kyrenia Region

## Highlights

**Mountains, forests and beaches**

The Kyrenia region offers a combination it is hard to beat, and will for most tastes make the best base for a holiday in North Cyprus. Endowed with mountains, forests and beaches, it boasts the most magnificent scenery on the island. Geographically central, it is well-placed for further exploration, and most of the two and three star sites lie within easy striking distance. The following table summarises the options:

| Half-day trips | Day Trips |
|---|---|
| St Hilarion | Vouni, Soli and Güzelyurt |
| Bellapais | Buffavento on foot |
| Buffavento by car | Nicosia, detailed |
| Nicosia, brief | Famagusta |
| Mountain monasteries | Salamis |
| Beaches to east and west | Kantara |
| | Karpas Peninsula (2 days) |

**Chic shopping**

The region offers a better choice of accommodation than either the Famagusta or Nicosia regions, from self-catering to 4 star, along with a wide range of restaurants from basic to ultra-chic, and surprisingly good shopping from supermarkets to boutiques.

The recent upsurge in investment has led to a rash of building projects. The creeping development, especially blocks of holiday flats, is sometimes unsightly and has made the fringes of Kyrenia and parts of the coastline to the west a bit tacky. That said, the town itself and much of the coast is, by Mediterranean standards, still relatively unspoilt.

**Timings**

Since the new road was built (with Saudi finance) Nicosia is just a 20 minute drive away, Ercan airport is a 40 minute drive and Famagusta is an hour and 10 minutes. From Kyrenia it takes 1 hour 45 minutes to reach Vouni, the westernmost point of interest, and four hours to reach Kastros at the easternmost tip of the Karpas.

**\*\*\***

# KYRENIA (GIRNE)

## Highlights

Kyrenia (Turkish Girne) is the prettiest town on the island, a tranquil seaside resort of the type that has all but died out in the Mediterranean. Its charming and tiny harbour, full of yachts and fishing boats, is framed by the colossal hulk of its **Crusader castle**. The promenade has been turned into a pedestrian zone, and the chic pavement restaurants conceal their kitchens behind elegant **Venetian facades**. With the backdrop of the jagged mountains behind and the calm sparkling sea in front, the **harbour** has an intoxicatingly serene atmosphere.

**Elegant facades**

Kyrenia's appeal is generally to the over 30's, those seeking refuge from the noise and dirt of the city. If breakfast on your balcony is disturbed by raucous backfiring, check before you turn to yell at yobs on motorbikes: the chances are it is grandad in his clapped-out Austin Cambridge taking little Mehmet to school. With a population of scarcely 7,000, it is by European standards no more than a village. There is one set of traffic lights, and the main street, **Hürriyet Caddesi**, can get quite busy, but once away from it, Kyrenia does feel more like a village, with narrow winding lanes and gentle pace. Along this main street and tucked into the side streets are shops offering a level of sophistication and choice that many a large town would be proud of. Turks from the mainland come to Kyrenia just for the shopping, as a lot of imported goods are either unavailable in Turkey or very expensive. **Enver's Pharmacy**, for example, could have been plucked straight out of Knightsbridge. Foreigners, especially British and Germans, drawn by

**Relaxed sophisti-cation**

its serenity and beauty, have bought homes here, both before and after 1974, either to retire, or perhaps as academics and scholars: though as Lawrence Durrell wrote in *Bitter Lemons* in 1956, 'Could one ever do any work with such scenery to wonder at?' He answered his own question by writing *Justine* here.

It is this relaxing quality that makes Kyrenia the ideal base for North Cyprus. When you return early from an excursion, or want a change from the beach, Kyrenia is an easy place to while away an hour or two strolling in the narrow cobbled alleys behind the harbour, exploring shops, markets and old houses, or stepping out for a brisk walk along the promenade and sea wall. Memorable evenings can be enjoyed in the restaurants and cafés, with the candlelight reflecting softly on the water and the gentle strumming of guitar music wafting out across the harbour.

**Memorable evenings**

Two hours should be set aside for visiting the castle and the Shipwreck Museum inside it. Besides the castle, Kyrenia's major monument, the town boasts a few small museums which can be visited in idle moments here and there as suits your itinerary. A little beyond the town, between the castle and the new port, you might also allow an hour for poking round the ancient quarries of Kyrenia, called Chrysokava, where a pair of simple rock churches used by early Christians can be seen.

**Timings**

**\*\*\* KYRENIA CASTLE**

## Highlights

This is the easiest of Cyprus' castles to visit, with no arduous climbs or vertiginous precipices. Inside, it is the best preserved of them all, and illustrates well the differences between Byzantine and Venetian military architecture.

The castle is open 8am-1pm, 2-5pm daily.

## Touring Kyrenia Castle

As you approach the castle from the harbour, the sheer power of the walls impresses. The huge round tower that confronts you is the work of the Venetians.

Such fortifications were their major legacy to Cyprus, for they always regarded it as a military outpost to protect and service their lust for trade.

The ticket office sits at the head of the **drawbridge**, and can be reached either by steps from the harbour, or from inland, via the little police station with its navy blue Landrovers. The moat you cross to reach the main gateway was full of water until 1400, and provided an inner protected harbour at times of war.

Once inside, the scale surprises, as you pass up a wide almost ceremonial ramp, built by the Venetians to facilitate rolling the cannon up into place on the walls. Above the inner gateway, carved into the stone,

**Impressive scale**

is the coat of arms of the Crusader Lusignans, the Frankish baronial family who ruled Cyprus for 300 years in the Middle Ages, and who remodelled much of the original Byzantine fort when they took it over in 1191. This **coat of arms** is the best preserved example on the island: it consists of three lions prancing on their hind legs, in contrast to the solitary Venetian winged lion to be found on the later walls and towers of Famagusta. Just beyond the inner gateway stands the **tomb of Sadık Pasha**, the Turkish Ottoman admiral to whom the Venetians surrendered in 1570, and who died later the same year.

The path leads on into a dauntingly large open courtyard with a somewhat neglected garden at one

**Crusader footballs**

end. Littering the ground are stones the size and shape of footballs, used in colossal catapult-like medieval weapons. Concerts are occasionally held in this sheltered courtyard. In 1961 Sir John Barbirolli performed here with the Hallé Orchestra. Today's performances are usually somewhat more modest.

A whole **maze of steps**, internal and external, interlink the Byzantine, Crusader and Venetian towers and ramparts of the castle. To the right (west) of the courtyard, dark foul-smelling steps set into the walls lead down into the dungeons, rarely empty in the complex series of plots and intrigues that make up the castle's past. The place was never taken by force throughout its history, though it was subjected to several lengthy sieges. The longest, in the 15th century, lasted nearly four years, and the unfortunate castle occupants were reduced to eating mice and rats.

**Rampart circuit**

If you enjoy heights and a certain amount of scrambling, it is possible to walk a complete circuit of the ramparts, thereby gaining the full panorama. The most photogenic stretch is definitely the northwestern tower and the western wall, with stunning views down into the harbour. Peeping out from the thickness of the wall by the northwest tower is the little **Byzantine chapel**, still with its four ancient marble columns, thought to have been taken from the old Roman town that now lies buried under modern Kyrenia. When built, in the 12th century, the chapel stood outside the castle walls, but the Venetians gave it an extra entrance and enclosed it in the 16th century within the tower. Hence its curious position today, where it simply serves as means of access to the tower.

**Kyrenian cowards**

Walking along the western wall inland towards the southwest tower you will get fine views over the rooftops of Kyrenia and the mountain pinnacles beyond. The tower itself is a remarkably advanced example of military design, built, like Famagusta's Martinengo Bastion, with three different heights of embrasure to allow three staggered levels of gunfire across the moat. These impressive **Venetian fortifications** are still in excellent condition, for they were never put to the test. In 1570, at the first confrontation since being completed around 1500, the Venetians at Kyrenia surrendered to the Turks without a single shot being fired. They had heard of the bloody fall of Nicosia, and their surrender spared them the devastating siege that Famagusta endured. Had they not surrendered, we would doubtless not be looking at such a well-preserved monument today. The rusting gun emplacements along the ramparts are the relics of the castle's modern role in the inter-communal fighting of this century.

Alongside this western wall are the roofless but still elegant remains of the Gothic style **royal apartments** of the castle, where the French Lusignan family resided at times of unrest or during their battles with the Genoese, their maritime rivals.

From the far southeast tower you can look down on to the rocky town beach tucked underneath the castle walls, with its own pretty **café terrace**. Pre-1974 this swimming spot was known as The Slab, and you had to be a member of the Country Club to use it. The Country Club is the building set up amid the greenery by itself above the bay, now called the **Halk Evi** or People's House. In the area in front of the Halk Evi and west towards the Anglican church, is the old Turkish cemetery. Excavations carried out here a few years ago revealed the elusive Roman town of Corineum, whose relics in the form of reused columns and capitals are visible here and there throughout the modern town.

**The original Kyrenia**

Tucked discreetly under the north (seaside) wall of the castle, are military patrol and gun boats, not visible from ground level except by walking out along the long harbour wall.

Built into a couple of the great halls along the eastern wall of the castle is the much praised **Shipwreck Museum**, where a 2,300 year old Greek trading vessel is on display, together with its complete cargo. It is the oldest ship yet recovered from the sea bed anywhere.

**The world's oldest ship**

There is an additional fee to enter, but it is worth it, since the museum is well laid out and is enhanced by the setting inside the lovely **Gothic halls** which form the main surviving domestic rooms of the castle. The museum was opened after the division of the island in March 1976, though most of the work was in fact completed pre-1974.

The ship was first discovered in 1965 by a Kyrenia sponge diver some 2km off the coast from the castle. Over the course of 1968 and 1969 a team of 50 underwater archaeologists from the University of Pennsylvania Museum raised the vessel systematically from the sea bed and it then took a further six years to reconstruct. Its cargo consisted of some 400 wine amphorae from Rhodes, 29 stone grain mills, lead weights and a staggering 9,000 almonds as food for the crew. It was these that enabled the carbon-dating of the ship. The reconstructed vessel is now in a

**Almonds for all**

separate temperature-controlled room. The Aleppo pine timbers had to be soaked in a preservative bath, then dried, and the hull was sheathed in lead. No skeletons were found, so the crew is thought to have swum to safety when the ship sank.

Also housed within the castle walls is the **Girne Department of Antiquities**, which took over custodianship of the castle in 1959.

In some of the castle's locked rooms, the Antiquities Department is keeping icons which were collected from churches in the Kyrenia area pre-1974 and stored here for safe keeping. Some of these are now on display for Archangel Michael church.

**EOKA and the British**

Under British rule, the castle was also used as a police barracks and training school, and as a prison for members of EOKA, the Greek Cypriot resistance movement. EOKA, the Nationalist Organisation of Cypriot Fighters, had begun in 1954, and from secret headquarters somewhere in the Troodos mountains, they organized a series of terrorist and sabotage attacks against British administration, to further their aim of union with Greece, or Enosis as this union was known. Pro-Enosis propaganda was concentrated in schools, where it was easy to sway feelings. Schoolteachers were mainly Greek-trained and full of Greek ideology. Although Enosis did not begin as an anti-British sentiment, it gradually became so, to the extent that anyone suspected of collaboration with the British was murdered. The Greek Orthodox church, encouraged by Archbishop Makarios, retained a strong role in the conflict, refusing to give the sacrament to those who assisted the British police or who betrayed information on EOKA fighters. In the view of impartial observers, the majority of the population was intimidated and uncertain, simply wanting the end of military rule and the return of the old peaceful lifestyle. The Turkish Cypriots felt threatened by the prospect of union with Greece, and

**Common destiny**

the seeds were sown for the inevitable inter-communal fighting. 'Greece and Turkey', as A E Yalman, editor of the Turkish newspaper *Vatan*, wrote in 1960, 'have a common destiny. They are condemned either to be to be good neighbours, close friends, faithful allies — or to commit suicide together.'

### *** KYRENIA HARBOUR

## Highlights

The harbour must be one of the most picturesque in the Mediterranean. Besides providing a fine setting for a range of eating places al fresco or indoors according to season, it also incorporates a number of curious relics of its ancient harbour, in with its modern one.

The harbour is beautiful at all times of day, but is maybe at its most bewitching at night. Many of the restaurants are open for food all day long.

### Touring Kyrenia harbour

The graceful horseshoe curve of Kyrenia's harbour is an even more tranquil spot since it was closed to traffic by a barrier at the west end (except for a few hours in the morning to allow deliveries). A fair proportion of the buildings enclosing the harbour are Venetian, tastefully restored to shops and restaurants on their ground levels, with apartments or the owner's accommodation above. The **tourist office** is itself such a restored house, with a cavernous stone vaulted interior.

**Venetian tourist office**

Above head height between what is now the Corner Bar and the Maribou Restaurant, you can see large stones jutting out with a hole in their centre. In the ancient harbour, ropes were threaded through these holes for hauling boats up on to the beach.

Sticking out of the water amongst the moored fishing boats and yachts, stands a semi-collapsed squat stone tower, approached by a crumbling causeway. On top of the tower is a smaller tower the size of a Roman column. This was the **old chain tower**, from which an iron chain was suspended across the harbour entrance to block hostile shipping. The chain, though huge, was but a tiny version of that used in Istanbul to control shipping in the Bosphorus. In the old wall that rises up behind the Café Chimera, careful observation will reveal a large **Gothic archway**, now blocked up. Before 1400, when the moat was still full, ships used to be dragged through this archway from the harbour into the castle moat for safety or simply for repair.

Strolling out along the harbour wall affords you the best view back of the castle and the difference in architectural styles is clearly visible. To the left (east) you have a good view for the first time of the taller Crusader tower, which was difficult to see from inside the castle or from the harbour front. Its high squared medieval crenellations and arrow slits were built with **Crusader** quite a different style of warfare in mind — catapults **arrows** and archery — from the later more advanced tower of **versus** the Venetians, round and squat, with no arrow slits **Venetian** but just a solitary gun port at sea level and others on **cannon** top for the newly invented cannon. From the very end of the harbour wall you can also view the eastern wall of the castle. The pathway underneath it is closed, a forbidden area because of the military gunboats moored nearby.

Walking away from the horseshoe harbour towards the Dome Hotel, you will notice a solitary granite **Roman column** beside the children's playground on the seafront promenade. It is something of a mystery, for though there are several Roman stone fragments to be found incorporated into churches or other buildings in Kyrenia, this is the only granite one. There is no indigenous granite in Cyprus, and this is the only piece of granite yet found in the whole Kyrenia area.

## ** KYRENIA TOWN

### Highlights

A stroll round Kyrenia town offers a relaxing break from the beach or ruin sightseeing. The pretty streets have a surprising range of shops, and souvenir hunting among them is a pleasure. Here and there you will come unexpectedly on an old mosque or church or ancient tower, a relic of the town walls.

Shops open at 8 or 9 am, often close for an hour from 1-2pm, and the majority then close at 5.30 or 6pm in the winter. In the summer they close from 1-

**Timings**  4pm, then reopen until 7.30 or 8pm. Distances are short, so a walk round the shops can be easily fitted in whenever you have the odd half hour to spare.

## Touring Kyrenia town

Medieval Kyrenia was a walled town, and today the narrow wiggling streets and alleys behind the harbour still retain a slightly medieval feel, the houses huddled on top of each other. The variety fascinates: one

**Intriguing variety**  moment you walk past a workshop where wood is crafted into furniture, the next you catch a glimpse on to a private arcaded courtyard with tumbling jasmine and bougainvillaea. The town walls themselves have been gradually dismantled and incorporated into other buildings, but you will still come across some of the towers tucked a little incongruously beside a butcher's shop or a supermarket. The most obvious **old tower** is the one in the western corner of the harbour, up a few steps close to the Tourist Office. The position of the others is shown on the map. The one beside the Municipal Market has now been converted to a crafts centre for the sale of traditional goods.

Close behind the harbour you will find Kyrenia's oldest mosque, the tiny **Djafer Pasha mosque**, frequented by a handful of faithful worshippers.

**Relaxed Islam**  Turkish Cypriots are not known for their religious fervour, and a fairly relaxed view of Islam is taken on the island. The mosque was built by and named after a Turkish general shortly after the Turkish takeover in 1570, and is a pleasant if unexciting example of early Ottoman architecture. Beside the mosque an ancient spring was converted to an area for the ritual ablutions before prayers and it is still here in the open street that the hand and foot washing takes place.

Flights of steps connect the streets and in the area behind the mosque you will come across some very splendid old buildings, once private residences for the governor and wealthy citizens, now converted to bars and restaurants, like The Club and the Set Pizza with its magnificent balustraded terrace.

Walking back towards the middle of the harbour curve, just one street inland, you come to the entrance of the **Folk Museum**, set in a typical 18th century house (open 8am-1pm, 2-4pm, closed weekends) overlooking the harbour to the front. The house need only detain you for 15 minutes and is of interest less for its display of domestic equipment and costumes than for the chance to see inside one of these three-storeyed old buildings. Diagonally opposite its entrance is Kyrenia's oldest church, c. 1500, the **Chrysopolitissa**, now closed, and with a curious walled-up Gothic arch.

**New icon museum**

The prominent bell-tower of the **Greek Orthodox church**, **Archangel Michael**, forms a landmark from many parts of town, set up as it is on a rocky outcrop. It was built in 1860, with the Turks' blessing, and the bell was even donated by a Turkish resident. The church was locked from 1974, until it reopened in 1991 as an icon museum to display some of the icons from the churches of the Kyrenia area, hitherto stored in the castle.

Today the only churches still open for worship are the **Anglican St Andrew's Church** behind the police station on a cliff by the southwest tower of the castle, and the **Roman Catholic Church** diagonally opposite the Dome Hotel. Anglican services are held at St Andrew's on Sundays with communion on Thursdays, and the Roman Catholic church holds a mass on the first Sunday of the month.

**Riddled with tombs**

Opposite the street from the Greek Orthodox church you can see **Byzantine catacombs** cut into the brown limestone cliffs, with the attractive Perge restaurant squatting on top of them. In the area between the Dome Hotel and the main shopping street inland, there are large numbers of these tombs, some 70 in all, the majority of them now covered by shops and modern buildings.

Today's population of Kyrenia, roughly 7,000, is similar to what it was before 1974. Many private houses were looted in the fighting and by 1976 only some 200 out of the original 2,500 British residents remained. Turks from the Limassol area were resettled here, and given land and property that had been Greek, in the same way that Greeks were given

Turkish property in the south in compensation for their losses in the north. Some mainland Turks have also been brought across, which is how the population level has been restored.

**Origins of the Turkish Cypriot community**

Settlement from the Turkish mainland was how the Turkish Cypriot community first began on the island. After the defeat of the Venetians in 1571, the Turkish Commander Lala Mustapha Pasha chose 12,000 infantry and 4,000 cavalrymen to stay behind as colonists. A further 22,000 decommissioned soldiers and their families also went to Cyprus, along with their livestock, tools for their crafts and all their possessions. They were given expatriate allowances and tax exemptions for the first three years to encourage them to settle, as was common practice by the Ottomans throughout their conquered territories. To help in the rebuilding and repopulating process, they favoured especially farmers, and thereafter a range of other skills like weavers, cobblers, tailors, masons, coppersmiths, miners etc. They also favoured families with young daughters. Many settlers came from the Black Sea coastal areas of Trabzon and Sinop, and the resettlement continued intermittently until the 18th century. By the time of the British administration in 1878, there were 95,000 Turkish Cypriots living on the island.

**Population changes**

Kyrenia's population in the past was subject to wild fluctuations depending on plagues, droughts and other disasters. In 1814 it was recorded that a mere 15 families lived in the town, all Greeks, and the ruling Turks would withdraw to the castle at night. From the 16th century, under the Ottoman administration, the population was fairly evenly balanced between Turks and Greeks. The Turks were traditionally landowners and farmers, while the Greeks were fishermen and shop owners. The Greeks tended to be the merchants. By 1900 the population had risen to some 1,500, and this then gradually increased as Kyrenia and the surrounding area became the favoured place of retirement for British colonial officials, living their lives of 'blameless monotony', as Lawrence Durrell put it in his *Bitter Lemons*. The British had taken on the administration of Cyprus from the Ottomans because it was of strategic importance, since the 1869 opening of the Suez Canal, in the protection of their trade route to India. Five years later however, when Britain was also in military occupation of Egypt, Cyprus ceased to be vital and was subsequently neglected, with little financial investment.

## \* CHRYSOKAVA: ROMAN QUARRIES

### Highlights

These quarries are quick and easy to visit when not closed by the military, and offer an unusual opportunity to see the ingenuity of earlier builders.

It is not a 'site' as such, so there is no ticket kiosk or opening hours. Avoid the midday heat in the summer, as there is no shade. It takes five minutes by car from Kyrenia or half an hour on foot from the castle. Allow an hour or so for a good look round.

### Touring Chrysokava

The ancient quarries of Chrysokava lie on the coast 1km to the east of Kyrenia castle, shortly before reaching the new Kyrenia port (Girne Turizm Limanı) where the new ferries and hydrofoil services run to the Turkish mainland. Those with the appropriate time, energy and ankles will enjoy the scramble round the rocky coastline from the castle and past the Turkish Maritime Martyrs Memorial.

**Easier route** The easier route however, is to drive out to Kyrenia's outskirts on the Famagusta road, then forking left just before the hospital (Hastahane). This road runs past the Castle Court Flats and the modern Turkish cemetery into an area of holiday flat developments on the rocky cliffs near the sea. Turning down the second tarmac road to the left after the cemetery, you drive towards the sea till you arrive at an open, rocky and treeless area in front of the new villas and flats, some 200m before the sea.

A little to the east is the new North Cyprus University College, opened in 1986, offering four year BSc degrees in Business Administration. The college is a fee-paying private institution, open to students from all nations, and all teaching is in English.

Leaving the car parked and walking on towards the sea you will now come upon five subterranean sunken areas in the cliffs, in some of which enterprising farmers have constructed plastic greenhouses to take advantage of the highly fertile soil in the quarry bottom.

**Limestone quarries**

It was from these quarries that limestone blocks were cut for the castle by the Crusaders and the later Venetians. The rock here lent itself so well to cutting that Byzantine Christians even built houses and churches here, as well as an ancient cistern to collect rainwater in the absence of springs.

Close to the sea at the edge of the easternmost of the quarries, a small **13th century chapel** was built, called Ayia Ekatorini, but this, alas, collapsed in 1988. A little further inland, a series of three quarries runs east west, two of which are interconnected by a

*The rock church at Chrysokava*

tunnel under a natural rock bridge. In the middle of one of these three is the most remarkable sight in the quarries, a small early **rock cut chapel** with traces of painting on its ceiling. Many of the other quarries have small niches and arches carved into their sides. With careful observation you can also find a quarried road which leads down to the remains of a **jetty**.

**Painted ceiling**

The rock here is the colour of sandstone, but is in fact limestone and hence more hardwearing. The quarry settlement was abandoned sometime in the 9th century probably because of lack of water supplies, and its desertion was speeded up by the waves of Arab raids that swept the coasts of Turkey and Cyprus at that time.

On the western edge of Kyrenia, past the Dome Hotel, on the headland in front of the Rocks Hotel are further quarries, and these ones were still in use in the 19th century.

### *** ST HILARION CASTLE

## Highlights

This castle and royal summer palace makes an exciting and mildly strenuous half day trip from Kyrenia. It is the best preserved of the three mountain-top Crusader castles of Cyprus and also the most romantic. 'Dieu d'Amour' was the name the Frankish knights bestowed upon it, and certainly from afar, its extravagantly crenellated walls and towers tumbling over the craggy hilltop evoke a fairy-tale vision of bygone chivalry. From within, the paths and steps wind up through the three castle sections, one superimposed on the other, and culminating in the royal apartments ingeniously sheltered in their own natural courtyard of rock. Rose Macaulay, author of the famous *Towers of Trebizond*, described it as 'a picture book castle for elf kings', and Walt Disney is said to have used it as the basis for his film set in *Snow White and the Seven Dwarfs*.

**Fairy-tale chivalry**

The path to the uppermost section of the castle is steep and slippery, and not suitable for anyone with wobbly legs or balance. One Canadian tourist slipped and fell to his death here in recent years. Choose appropriate footwear.

**Timings**

The castle is open from 8.30am to 5pm daily and tickets are bought from the guardian at the entrance. The other castles of Buffavento and Kantara, incidentally, have no guardian, and consequently no entry fee or opening hours. A drive of 15 minutes from Kyrenia brings you to the car park at the foot of St Hilarion, and from here the walk up to the summit takes a good half hour. You should allow at least two hours to explore all the different levels of the castle. There is no restaurant, though simple refreshments (coffee, tea, soft drinks and sweets) are on sale both outside at the ticket kiosk and inside the castle at the Great Hall. The energetic could carry a picnic to the 732m summit.

## Touring St Hilarion Castle

From Kyrenia you take the main road out towards Nicosia (Turkish Lefkoşa), and as you leave the town behind, you can already pick out the distinctive shape of the Hilarion peak above you a little to the right. It was Durrell who first used the word 'Gothic' to describe the Kyrenia range, and their sharp pinnacles do lend them a fine Gothic silhouette. The Troodos on the other hand, rounder and more rolling, are more naturally allied to the domes of Byzantine inspiration.

**Sharp pinnacles**

The much improved road network of the north is now such that a drive of just ten minutes brings you to the turn-off for St Hilarion, marked by a yellow sign to the right, shortly before the summit of the Nicosia pass. From here, after appearing to double back on itself, the narrow tarmac road winds for 2-3km (1-2 miles) and you will catch glimpses above of a soldier perched on a lofty crag, gun poised. He reveals himself on closer inspection to be made of metal. On the drive up your eye may also have been caught by a prominent white building alone on its crag among the thickly forested hills towards Bellapais — not a magnificent private villa, but a military headquarters. The military is never far away in North Cyprus, and it is as well to accustom yourself to the idea and regard it as an interesting extra dimension to the island's sights. As the approach road levels out and the castle comes into view, the track that branches off to the right leads to a military camp. On a large flat terrace to the left of the road is its rifle range, appropriately enough, for it was here that the knights held jousts and tournaments, watched by the ladies of the court waving coloured favours from the battlements.

**Military jousting ground**

The tarmac road terminates in a small car park with a simple **open-air café** and the ticket kiosk. Tickets here, as almost everywhere, cost TL1,000. To the west you will notice the dirt road continuing along the ridge of the mountains as it heads off to reach Karşıyaka. There is also a footpath from here down to the pretty village of Karmi (Turkish Karaman). The fact that the Karşıyaka drive of 29km (18 miles) takes at least one and a half hours is an indication of the state of the track, but for those with the time, the bumps are amply compensated for by the spectacular **mountain scenery** and abundant wildlife. See page 46. A hired saloon car can manage quite well unless there has been recent heavy rain.

**Diverting mountain drive**

By taking a picnic, a morning visit to the castle could be followed by this drive, thereby turning the outing into a day trip. Halfway along the track is a crossroads forking left for Akçiçek and right for Lapta, but you continue straight on for Karşıyaka. The final stretch from Mt Kıvanç down to join the tarmac road is the most difficult. To the right of the road above Karşıyaka you can spot a heavily ruined monastery.

Back at St Hilarion, the first section of the ascent through the castle now begins up well-laid steps and concrete paths. The **main gate and outer walls** were built originally by the Byzantines in the 11th century for extra defence, and these lowest parts were for the men-at-arms and the horses. In the many long sieges of medieval times this area and its cisterns were invaluable. The castle had its exposure to modern warfare too, serving in 1964 as a stronghold for Turkish Cypriots. Such were the castle's defences,

**The ascent begins**

even in ruin, that a garrison of boys was able to ward off the Greek attack. The Turkish army still used the castle until relatively recently, before moving out to their camp along the ridge.

As the path climbs up it passes one of the **cisterns**, still in use, built up against the wall, and at the first corner where the path bends and forks to the right, you can see the **stables** where the animals were kept.

**Monastic origins**

After a few minutes' climb you reach the **main gatehouse**, a huge and powerful structure which originally closed with a drawbridge. Entering the passage, a set of steps leads off to the **church**, quite well-preserved and still with traces of **12th century paintings** on the south (car park) side of the wall. Some restoration work was done here in 1959. In size it is larger than you would expect for a castle chapel, and this is because it belonged originally to a 10th century monastery built here by the Byzantines to honour St Hilarion, a hermit who had fled to Cyprus from the Holy Land to escape persecution. He died here in a nearby cave. An old man, 'unclean in person but very holy', he sought out refuge in the mountain, with its ample water supplies. Cypriot peasantry has long believed in evil spirits, 'kalikantzaroi' as they call them, which take weird and wonderful forms and have to be appeased at certain times of year by being thrown freshly baked honey doughnuts. The demons

**Demons and doughnuts**

who, by popular account, had until then held possession of this mountain-top, watched the hermit's arrival with dismay and conspired to drive him off with hideous noises. His hearing was such, however, that he merely thanked them for welcoming him with music and settled down to his solitary life, leaving the nonplussed demons to look elsewhere for their doughnuts.

The area all around the church was originally the monastery, and the series of rooms to the north and east of it were the **refectory, cellars and kitchen**, and a belvedere. The **fine old refectory**, the largest room in this group by far, was used in Lusignan Crusader times as a banqueting hall, and has now been restored as a modest café selling tea and coffee, soft drinks and sweets. The affable owner also has a good range of souvenirs, including St Hilarion honey, elaborately sugared fruits, carved wooden animals, books, cards and even a selection of old prints. The echoing walls and huge vaulted ceiling and rafters of the hall preserve an atmosphere of bygone days, with its smoke-blackened fireplace at the far end. Doors lead on to its narrow vertiginous **balcony** with a splendid panorama down over Kyrenia and the coast. In good weather this makes an excellent resting place, and for those who relish heights, chairs can be brought out on to the balcony. On clear days, especially in winter, the snow-covered Taurus mountains of mainland Turkey can be seen, some 100km (60 miles) distant. Immediately below is another series of rooms, thought to be barracks built for the Crusader knights in the 14th century. They are best reached by the stone steps that lead down from the main path just beyond the refectory, and are curious in that their floors follow the contours of the natural bedrock below. Do not be tempted to ascend the rickety wooden staircase at the far end tower here, as no maintenance work has been done for some years and it is decidedly unsafe.

**Refectory with a view**

From the refectory in the central, middle section of the castle, you now continue to the uppermost and in many ways the most intriguing part, the **royal apartments and watchtowers**. The path zigzags steeply up, sometimes on loose earth, sometimes on uneven rock steps. In the heavy rains and floods of 1968 it was washed away completely, and access to the castle summit was impossible. Just as the path begins, notice below you to the right a huge open cistern designed to collect winter rainfall.

**Tricky path**

At the top of the path you now enter the royal area by passing through a **Crusader archway** guarded by a tower. Heavily overgrown with trees and bushes, and strung across with a rotting rope walkway, a relic of the Turkish army's recent occupation, this area was the main courtyard, cleverly sheltered by being wedged between the twin peaks of the summit. These peaks gave the mountain its first name of Didymos (Greek for twin), from which the non Greek-speaking

**Royal summit**

*The Queen's Window, Castle of St Hilarion*

Crusaders arrived at the corruption Dieu d'Amour. The tumble-down buildings immediately to your right on entering are the **royal kitchens and waiting rooms**. In the centre of the courtyard you may stumble across, but hopefully not into, a **stagnant cistern** sunk into the rock, and beyond it, at the farthest end, are the royal apartments themselves, closing off the western side of the courtyard.

To reach these you follow the little path straight on through the undergrowth. The staircase which used to lead up to the first floor gallery on the south side has recently caved in, but that on the northern (sea) side is still safe, if somewhat overgrown. From it you emerge on to what is certainly the most evocative spot in the castle, a partly collapsed but elegant gallery, still retaining two Gothic tracery windows, the further one with charming stone window seats on either side. Popularly known as the **Queen's Window**, it is here that Queen Elinor is said to have sat, the Dynasty-style scheming queen of the Lusignans. Today the view over to the west is a spectacular one, with the little white picture-book village of **Karaman** in the foreground. This is now an expatriate village, formerly Greek Karmi, leased by the Ministry of Tourism to foreigners wishing to restore and live in old-style village houses.

**The scheming Queen's window seat**

Returning to the front part of the courtyard, the sure-footed can now climb the rugged steps with their wobbly iron railing and clamber along the ramparts and ruined tower to the southern peak, the highest point at 732m.

Just outside the courtyard area as you begin the descent, another set of rough steps leads off to the right to ascend the 14th century **Prince John's Tower**, a powerfully built watchtower on a rocky crag. It was from here that the gullible Prince John of Antioch in 1373 flung his faithful Bulgarian guards to their death, after receiving a fabricated warning about them from the scheming Queen Elinor. All but one were smashed on the rocks below and it was he who survived to tell the tale.

**A gory end**

In the structure of the castle, each of the three defensive sections was self-supporting, with its own cisterns and supply depots. All of the three castles in the Kyrenia range, St Hilarion, Buffavento and Kantara, were originally built as defence from Arab raids. From the 7th to the 10th centuries, the Arabs launched a succession of raids on Cyprus and all

**Arab raids**

along the coast of Turkey. The worst was that conducted in 806 by the Caliph Haroun ar-Rashid of One Thousand and One Nights' fame, in which the Arabs ravaged much of the island and abducted 16,000 as prisoners, including the archbishop and many other ecclesiastics. The goal of the raids was booty and prisoners, never to conquer and rule. The Arab armies still had many Bedouin in whom the tradition of 'raiding' (Arabic — ghazwa) was deeply rooted as a way of life. With the fighting for the Arab empire largely over, they had to find an alternative outlet for their energies and these raids were sanctioned by their leaders as a convenient method of keeping the armies fit and trained. The continuing raids had a marked effect on the population distribution, causing people to leave the coast and move inland to the hills.

St Hilarion castle served as a place of refuge and summer residence for the island's kings for some 400 years after this. It was not only to escape the heat of Nicosia that they came here, but sometimes also to escape great plagues. In the summer of 1349 the Black Death swept the island and the royal entourage bid a hasty retreat from Nicosia to the safe and healthy heights of Hilarion. Estimates of the number of people who died range from a quarter to half the island's population. The castle has, like its sisters Buffavento and Kantara, been a ruin since the 16th century, when the merchants of Venice, whose preoccupations always lay with the sea, methodically dismantled it to deter any troublesome insurrections that might arise in the island's interior and thus distract them from their trading activities.

**Escape from the Black Death**

'Happy is the country that has no history' runs the saying. Cyprus, Gordon Home's 'unhappy shuttle-cock', has too much. Its geographical location, stepping stone to the east from the western viewpoint, and to the west from the eastern viewpoint, has condemned it always to be the victim of predatory powers. Throughout its long past, Cyprus raised revolts against its rulers of the day, but they were nearly always quashed. Only on two occasions before

1960 did Cyprus experience independence. The first was in 367BC under the first king of the island, Evagoras, and the second was in 1184 under Isaac Comnenus.

Independence was, however, not necessarily any better for the Cypriots themselves, and it was in fact under the despotic rule of Isaac Comnenus that they suffered especially. Yet by a twist of fate, the rashness of this despot led to the Crusaders becoming rulers of the island. Cyprus was ruled at that time from Constantinople, by a Byzantine official sent to the island as local governor. Even so, the island continued to be unceremoniously raided, three times in the 12th century, first by Raymond of Chatillon, then by Egyptian bandits, then by Raymond Prince of **Isaac the** Antioch. Isaac Comnenus was the nephew of the **despot** Byzantine emperor, and after a family dispute, he fled to Cyprus and had himself proclaimed, through force and guile, the ruler of the island. His tyrannical seven year rule was thus chronicled: 'The island groaned beneath this scourge of fate, and he reduced the Cypriots to such a state of despair that all were ready to welcome anything which afforded a means of escape from such tyranny'. He starved and robbed the wealthy, murdered and ravished young virgins at whim.

**Enter King** His violence and temper met their match however, **Richard** in the person of Richard the Lionheart. Richard was on his way to the Holy Land in the Third Crusade in 1191 when some of his ships were wrecked off the Cypriot coast. Isaac Comnenus rushed to the scene and seized the booty. In the process however, he unwisely insulted two of the passengers, Berengaria, Richard's betrothed, and Joanna, his favourite sister. Enraged at Isaac's affrontery, Richard, who had had no intention of conquering Cyprus, pursued Comnenus and unceremoniously defeated him. Isaac's daughter was locked up in St Hilarion. Richard despatched his knights to take the rest of the island and in turn helped himself to large quantites of booty, as was customary. He stayed on the island long enough to marry the dark-eyed Berengaria, daughter of the King of

Navarre, and one tradition recounts that Isaac, gift wrapped in gilt chains, was brought to the queen as a wedding present.

**From the wolf to the bear**

Though generally presented as a hero, Richard was in fact not much different to Cyprus' previous rulers. The Archbishop of Sinai, chronicling events in 1766, described him as a 'bloodthirsty beast', lamenting that the poor Cypriots 'had escaped the wolf to fall into the jaws of the bear'.

On leaving the island, Richard sold it to the Knights Templar for 100,000 byzants (the medieval gold currency of Europe), to raise money for his army and the crusade. The knights, however, found it more of a handful than they bargained for, and after only a year they besought Richard to buy it back. The English king had already received nearly half the sale price and did not wish to lose his money. Instead, he persuaded Guy de Lusignan, a Frankish nobleman who had been King of Jerusalem before it was lost to Saladin, to take it on in compensation for the loss of the kingdom of Jerusalem. Guy accepted, and his family retained the kingship of the island for the next three centuries, until 1489.

Lusignan's reign was always feudal in style, and did not represent an improvement for the Cypriots themselves. They were serfs with no rights or privileges, working the land and heavily taxed to pay for the extravagances of the nobles. Some were even bartered by their masters in exchange for dogs or horses.

**Greek orthodoxy crushed**

Also subjugated at this time was the Greek Orthodox Church of Cyprus, scorned by the French-speaking Latin Catholic rulers. Its treasures were robbed and its bishops burnt as heretics when they refused to bow to Catholic dominance and recognize the Pope in Rome as head of all Christendom. The appointment of an orthodox archbishop was banned, and it was in these centuries that the Greek Orthodox monasteries, hidden away in the mountain ranges, were established. Cyprus had long been a refuge for Christianity during difficult times in the Holy Land, and when the last Christian stronghold of Acre fell in

1191, Cyprus took on the role of Latin Christianity's easternmost outpost, becoming the trading centre of the eastern Mediterranean, and bringing its rulers much wealth and prosperity. The relics of this prosperity are left to us today in the cathedrals of Nicosia and Famagusta, the castles of St Hilarion, Buffavento and Kantara, and the unrivalled Bellapais Abbey.

### *** BELLAPAIS ABBEY

### Highlights

The beauty of Bellapais is legendary. When Lawrence Durrell bought a house here, he felt 'guilty of an act of fearful temerity in trying to settle in so fantastic a place'. Set in the mountains just ten minutes above Kyrenia, a visit to this magnificent 14th century Crusader abbey with its fabulous location and pervasive atmosphere of calm, is a must.

**Fabulous location**

Those who knew Bellapais before the 1950s speak disparagingly of the encroaching commercialisation of the abbey. There are indeed a handful of cafés and souvenir shops beside the abbey, and even a restaurant inside it, but they can be counted on the fingers of one hand, and the narrow streets of the village will scarcely permit more than this. Parking can sometimes be a little tricky as a result, though there is also a large open parking area just beyond the abbey. Beware of sitting under the famous 'Tree of Idleness', an ancient mulberry by the abbey entrance, lest you are struck down with the indolence for which the villagers are famed. Bellapais, Durrell was told, was synonymous with laziness and the villagers lived for so long that even the gravedigger was out of a job.

**Tree of Idleness**

At least two hours should be allowed for the visit, starting from Kyrenia, and the most special time is sunset, when the place is alive with the glowing silhouettes of arches. 'The dawns and the sunsets in Cyprus,' wrote Durrell, 'are unforgettable — better even than those of Rhodes which I always believed were unique in their slow Tiberian magnificence.' Durrell himself would frequently see the dawn, for

*Bellapais Abbey*

when he ran out of money for renovating his house, he took a job teaching English in a Nicosia school which meant he had to get up at 4.30am.

Entry to the abbey is by ticket and the kiosk is open 9am-6.30pm. If you are especially fortunate, you might coincide with one of the concerts occasionally held in the abbey refectory: a more picturesque musical backdrop is hard to imagine. Later, after a stroll, you could stay on for dinner at one of the nearby restaurants, and soak up the abbey, illuminated in its own surrealistic halo. Sipping wine on the terrace, you may wonder if you are hallucinating as a tractor trundles by towing a grand piano.

## Touring Bellapais Abbey

Climbing the 5km (3 mile) drive from Kyrenia through olive and carob groves and ever-increasing development, few are prepared for the vista that hits them as they round the last corner before Bellapais village. There, rising up from the mountain on its natural terrace, like a mirage, is the Gothic masterpiece of the island, and indeed of all the Levant. Rarely has a place so lived up to its name, for this remarkable 14th century abbey is imbued with a sense of tranquillity and peace so powerful it is almost tangible.

**Gothic mirage**

The road winds through the narrow streets of Bellapais village to reach the tiny square in front of the abbey. From here the path leads in from the ticket kiosk to the abbey enclosure through a pretty and colourful **garden**, to what was once the abbey kitchen, and is now a **restaurant and café**, tastefully tucked into the side and with excellent views of the abbey and down over the coastline. In the abbey courtyard, the fine pencilled cypress trees, 'emblems of grief and eternity' as eminent travel writer Colin Thubron called them, were only planted in 1940, but now they are home to hundreds of sparrows whose incessant chirping is usually the only sound to greet you as you enter.

Thoughtfully placed at the refectory door, by the

lovely tracery windows of the cloister, lies a fine white **marble sarcophagus** of the 2nd century AD, carved with dainty figures and foliage. Here, the fastidious monks would wash their hands before meals. The first monks here were Augustinians, displaced from their custody of the Holy Sepulchre Church in Jerusalem by the arrival of Saladin in 1187. Fleeing with them were some canons of the order of St Norbert, whose white habits lent Bellapais its other name of The White Abbey. Initially, the strictness of the abbey was exemplary, and converts were drawn from far afield.

**Conflicts of the spirit**

Gradually, however, worldly values began to infiltrate. The mellow beauty of the abbey was not the natural bedfellow of asceticism, as Thubron wryly observed on his first visit: 'The spirit here feels more like a ripe fruit than a soldier of God.' Stories of the monks' misdeeds gathered momentum, as they took not just one, but two and three wives, and would accept only their own sons as novices. By the time the Genoese arrived in 1373, the abbey was ripe for pillaging, and much of its treasure was abducted. The Ottoman invasion of the 16th century destroyed more of the abbey, but the Turks allowed the Greeks to use the church after the monks were driven out. The abbey church in fact continued to be used as the village church until 1974.

**Bellapais swells**

Prior to the Ottoman takeover, the village of Bellapais had scarcely existed, but its numbers were swelled by the sudden influx of Greeks fleeing Kyrenia. The daughters of the monks also played their role in the growing population.

The abbey itself, though the church was still used, was a ruin from the 16th century onwards, for what the Turks did not destroy, the arriving Greeks plundered as a most convenient quarry for building their new houses. Early travellers observed cows grazing in the cloisters. The British Army made its contribution by using the place as a military hospital after 1878, cementing over the refectory floor.

This **refectory**, with its lovely fan vaulted ceiling

**Dining in style**

and perfect proportions, must have been one of the finest dining halls in the east. Carved into the thickness of the wall is a pulpit from which the monks were addressed throughout meals. High on the end wall, a **rose window** casts an attractive patterned light. On the marble lintel above the entrance, are three well-carved sets of **coats of arms** — the prancing lions of the Lusignans on the right, Jerusalem in the centre, and the royal quarterings of Cyprus on the left.

The **abbey church**, which runs the length of the cloister on the opposite side of the refectory, is still used now for occasional services, and has recently been opened to the public again, revealing the lovely iconostasis and wooden carving on the pulpits. Pre-1974 accounts describe it as remarkably unchanged from its original 13th century structure, apart from the iconostasis which was added by the Greek Orthodox church in the 16th century.

**Dormitories with a view**

There are two ways up to the **abbey roof**: one is a set of stairs near the church entrance on the garden side, and the other is a long straight vaulted staircase running up on the church side of the cloister. This latter was the nightstair, used by the monks to come down from their dormitories at midnight for prayers. Today the roof forms an excellent viewing and vantage point from which to look down on the cloister with its melancholy cypresses and colourful garden, and across to the sea beyond.

From the car park behind the abbey to the east, you have the best view of the heavily ruined **undercroft** or work room with its simple vaulting and damaged rose window to the north. Beside it in the southeast corner, is the **chapter house**, used like an administration office for the abbey, which merits closer inspection because of its eccentric Gothic stone carving, featuring wriggling sirens, monsters embracing or fighting, and a monkey and cat in the foliage of a pear tree.

The village of Bellapais still boasts a fair number of foreigners among its residents, especially in the newer villas that have grown up on the outskirts. Its

**Durrell's
posh
house**

closeness to Kyrenia and natural beauty and tranquillity make it an obvious choice, and its image and popularity were certainly enhanced by Lawrence Durrell's purchase of a house here in 1953, and his subsequent book about the island and its troubles, *Bitter Lemons*, published in 1957. Durrell's house still stands at the top of the steep road that runs up from the Tree of Idleness, opposite the 1953 water trough, and is now the poshest house in the village, lovingly restored and superbly maintained by the current owner. The well-designed Ambelia village self-catering complex was built nearby in 1973, and more recently the sprawling village of Ozanköy beneath Bellapais has also become fashionable for foreigners purchasing and converting traditional homes.

## * WEST FROM KYRENIA

### Highlights

A day or two spent trundling off to the west of Kyrenia offers the chance to see a different kind of Cypriot scenery, notably the highly fertile plain of Güzelyurt (former Morphou) with its citrus and banana plantations. There are many good swimming beaches, and there is a wide variety of sites to see, ranging from the sultry hilltop Persian palace of Vouni, to the Bronze Age sanctuary at Pighades, to Roman fish tanks at Lapta.

**Good
beaches**

Once you have passed the Celebrity Hotel complex some 14km (9 miles) west of Kyrenia, there is no further hotel accommodation of tourist standard available. Restaurant facilities are also limited, though there is a cluster of beach restaurants between Soli and Vouni. None of the antiquities are in themselves spectacular, but they are all from different periods and offer an interesting diversity.

**Itinerary planning**

Distances are mercifully short in northern Cyprus, and driving at a gentle pace it takes no more than an hour to reach Güzelyurt, and a further 45 minutes to arrive at the Persian palace of Vouni. This rocky summit is the westernmost place to visit, and the best policy on a day's outing from Kyrenia is to drive first to this, then to work your way back eastwards. That way, if you run out of daylight and still have some places to visit, they will at least be closer to home for subsequent visits. In the summer months it is perfectly realistic to make leisurely morning visits to Vouni and Soli, then to take lunch at one of the beach restaurants near Soli (at Yedidalga). After lunch there will still be time to see Lefke, Güzelyurt, Pighades and probably Lapta on the way home. In winter, with shorter daylight hours, the afternoon itinerary may have to be curtailed, as it is too dark after 5pm to do any sightseeing.

## Touring west from Kyrenia

Following the above suggestion, the description given here starts with a brief account of the route westwards to Vouni, then gives the site details starting from Vouni and working eastwards back towards Kyrenia. As throughout northern Cyprus, the roads are in good condition, and there is blissfully little traffic. The towns are clearly signposted.

**Traffic-free driving**

The road first follows the thin coastal strip beneath the Kyrenia range for 20km (12 miles) or so, before it then begins to climb as it winds inland through wooded hillsides. Leaving the valleys behind, you have a fine view below to a new dam, one of many which the North Cypriots are now building to harness the water that is lost in a flash after a heavy downpour: no river in Cyprus flows all year round and water is a scarce resource. For most of the year it comes from the mains for only two hours a day, and in July and August sometimes not at all. Residents and hotels get round this by having extremely large tanks on the roof.

At the top of the climb you arrive at Çamlıbel (Greek Myrtou), a heavily garrisoned town, where there is a major fork in the road: straight on to Nicosia, and right to Güzelyurt and Lefke. The road straight on is the one you need to take to visit Pighades, just 2km (1 mile or so) away, on the return journey, but for now, you fork right.

Leaving Çamlıbel on its hilltop, the road drops down into the adjacent valley. Güzelyurt is set in the heart of this vast and fertile river plain, the centre for the island's citrus plantations. Some 80% of the island's citrus groves were concentrated here, and in the first few years after 1974, the Turkish Cypriots had neither the manpower nor the expertise to tend them. Many trees died from neglect or disease, but by 1980 the situation was under control, and exports of citrus fruits began an upward trend. Sunzest, the juice and canning factory of Asil Nadir, Turkish Cypriot ex-millionaire, is conspicuous at the town's outskirts.

**Citrus centre**

A fine **pink steam engine** just to the left of the road heralds your arrival at Güzelyurt. This curiosity is a leftover of the line built by the British which used to run from Famagusta via Nicosia to Morphou. The last train ran in 1951. Continuing straight along the main road, you reach the centre of town with the unmistakable Byzantine dome of the **Ayias Mamas church** and the municipal museum beside it, both set in the centre of a huge roundabout, and both described in detail on the return journey. The forks to the left from the roundabout lead back towards Nicosia, but you continue straight on, following signs for Lefke.

**Railway relic**

Güzelyurt, its population of some 10,000 making it North Cyprus' third biggest town after Nicosia and Famagusta, has the pleasant feel of a rural market garden town. It is almost entirely low-rise, and buildings higher than two storeys are a rarity.

From Güzelyurt the drive on through lush

plantations takes a further half hour to reach the sweep of Güzelyurt Körfezi (Morphou Bay) with its **distinctive iron jetties**, relics of the copper mining operations. Ships would tie up alongside these jetties and be loaded with copper for export, mainly to West Germany. Copper was Cyprus' most important natural resource, and the Greek name for it, 'kupros', is even thought to be taken from the name of the island. Cyprus was known throughout ancient times for her copper, supplying the Egyptian pharoahs and producing more than any other Mediterranean country. The rich mines here of Skouriotissa and Mavrovouni were first worked by the ancient Greeks and then the Romans, but after that lay disused for centuries until they were reopened in 1923. The Cyprus Mines Corporation, an American outfit, worked the mines until partition, when the ore was nearly exhausted anyway. Their supervisors marvelled at the extent of the Roman diggings, and the depth of their galleries and shafts, especially in view of the lack of ventilation. Slaves were used, of course, to work the mines, so safety standards were hardly a consideration. In Roman times Christians from Palestine who refused to renounce their faith, were also sent down the mines. Careful observation of the landscape will reveal it to be largely composed of Roman slagheaps, for they are said to have left more than a million tons of slag behind. 'Our Lady of the Slag Heaps' is one rough translation of Skouriotissa.

**Rich copper mines**

**Roman slagheaps**

Shortly after the mining sites, but before the village of Yedidalga, the Roman theatre and basilica of Soli lie on a hillside just 200m inland from the road. The signposting here is not good, and you must look out for the makeshift ticket office raised up with SOLI painted on its corrugated iron sides in clumsy red letters.

Vouni too, about 8km (5 miles) further west, is not signposted at this stage, but you should just continue along the coast road, always bearing right when there is a choice. Until recently it was necessary to stop at the police station in Yedidalga to obtain a permit to visit Vouni, but this formality has now been dropped and you can proceed on your way with no worries.

First the road passes a cluster of beach restaurants west of Soli, where you can eat and swim, before a steep winding ascent begins of a colossal hilly outcrop on the sea edge. Vouni palace lies on the summit of this outcrop. Near the foot of the hill, about halfway between Soli and Vouni, is the shell of a modern Greek church built in a sheltered nook to the right of the road, but badly destroyed inside. It appears never to have been completed and is covered inside and out with the vain exhortation 'Please keep tidy'. Most mosques in Greek Cyprus are, by contrast, kept locked and clean, but the record for tolerance is poor on both sides: 117 mosques were destroyed between 1955 and 1974 by zealous Greek Cypriots.

**Beach interlude**

At the foot of the Vouni hill, the main road continues westwards to the village of Yesilırmak, just beyond which is another simple **beach restaurant**. This is the westernmost point you can reach before the edge of North Cypriot territory, though some 8km (5 miles) further west, inaccessible and surrounded by Greek Cypriot territory, is the curious Turkish Cypriot pocket of Erenköy (Greek Kokkina). Today only troops live in this fiercely Turkish Cypriot enclave, all the original villagers having been evacuated to Yeni Erenköy on the Karpas peninsula. These villagers had bravely resisted an attack by General Grivas and 3,000 Greek soldiers in 1964 and were supported in their struggle by student volunteers who included a young Rauf Denktash, the TRNC's president.

**Military pocket**

Having arrived at the westernmost point, the site descriptions now begin from Vouni eastwards.

## * VOUNI

### Highlights

This is the only Persian palace in Cyprus, indeed in the Mediterranean, and it lies on a spectacular hilltop overlooking the sea. However, the remains of the palace are scant, and the imagination has to be called into play.

The ticket kiosk is open from 9am-1pm and 2-5pm daily. There is no refreshments stall here, so bring your own, especially liquid in the summer months. Vouni is a good spot for a picnic. Allow 45 minutes for a full walk round.

## Touring Vouni

A makeshift signpost announces **Vouni Palace** only once during the steep drive up, and then once more at the final junction, where you leave the main road and fork off to the right to reach the ticket office and car park on the summit. The dizzy views down to the sea are stunning, with the rocky island of Petra Tou **The first** Limniti in the foreground. It was on this island that **Cypriots** Cyprus' earliest inhabitants lived, and traces of a pre-Neolithic settlement were found there by the same Swedish expedition in the 1920s that excavated Vouni and Soli. Local folklore holds this is the rock (as indeed are all the small rock islands off Cyprus' shore) that the hero Dighenis tossed on to the ships of the Arab raiders of the 7th century.

The name Vouni means mountain peak, and it was built on this summit specifically to dominate and spy on the city kingdom of Soli down below, which had at that time aligned itself with the Greeks in a revolt against Persia. The palace was only in use for some 70 years, for in 380BC it was destroyed by fire and not lived in again.

Reduced today to little more than its foundations, the 5th century BC palace of Vouni may disappoint at first. Do not dismiss it too quickly though, for if you take the trouble to walk round slowly, you will be surprised how it can be transformed by careful **Hints of** observation and a little imagination into a magnificent **the exotic** royal residence. Ruined but gracious walkways, broad stairways and ample courtyards all hint at the opulent oriental lifestyle enjoyed here, and the **elaborate water system** is a marvel of 5th century BC engineering. Everywhere there are ingeniously cut channels and very deep wells, ensuring running water in all the main rooms. In the extreme northwest corner, near where the sign Gentlemen and Ladies

**Early
sauna**

announces the current facilities, there is a **water closet** beside a deep cistern, which in its day was probably far more luxurious than its modern counterpart could ever aspire to be. Lower down the hill are the **baths**, with one of the earliest known **saunas**. There were 137 rooms in all.

The path from the ticket office leads first straight into the area identified as the **royal apartments**, and from these a broad flight of seven steps leads down into the huge open **courtyard** which is the generally photographed view of Vouni. At its farthest end stands the strange carved stone stele which resembles an altar but was in fact designed to hold a **windlass** over the cistern well head. In the bulbous centre of the stone is an unfinished likeness of Athene.

The Swedish excavators made a series of finds in the palace that testified to the lavish lifestyle of the

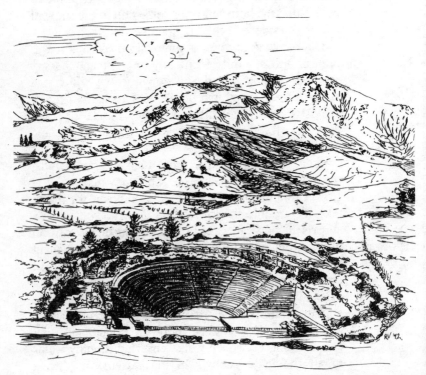

*The theatre at Soli*

**Hidden
treasure**

occupants. As well as **statues and bronzes** they discovered quantities of silver and gold treasure in the form of bracelets, bowls and coins. One local story tells of noblemen dining here and leaving their silver spoons behind, and villagers still refer to it as 'the eating place of the lords'. Much silver treasure was found in a terracotta jar that seemed to have been deliberately hidden under a staircase. Some of this treasure, including Persian-style snake head bracelets, can be seen in the Cyprus Museum of Greek Nicosia.

Beyond the palace area, at the highest point of the hill, stands a military trigonometry point, 250m above the sea, and nearby are the scant remains of a **temple to Athena** where the Swedish excavators found several sculptures, notably an endearing bronze cow, now also in the Cyprus Museum.

The serene and lovely location encourages much wildlife. Lizards up to a foot long leap around on the walls and butterflies sun themselves gaily in sheltered corners. All around, the yellow aromatic Johanniskreuz bush flourishes, well known for its stomach-calming qualities when drunk as a tea.

## * SOLI

### Highlights

The Roman site of Soli boasts the best preserved mosaic and marble floor in northern Cyprus in its basilica, and nearby beach restaurants offer a pleasant stop for lunch and a swim.

The site lacks grandeur and its setting, though raised up overlooking the bay, is a bit scruffy and uninspiring. The theatre is the only other monument to have been excavated besides the basilica, and has been rather over-restored.

The ticket kiosk is open the standard 9am-5pm and about 45 minutes should be allowed for a tour. There are no refreshments available, and Soli is not a particularly good picnic spot.

### Touring Soli

Coming from Vouni, you must look out for the Soli

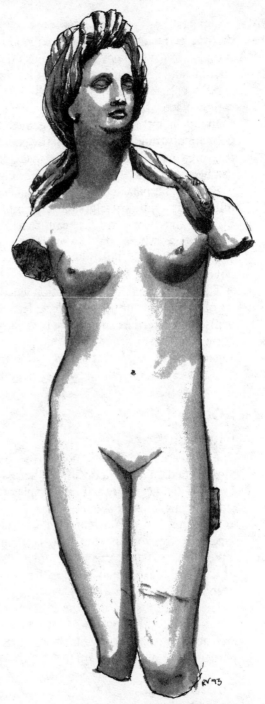

*Armless Aphrodite found at Soli, 1st century BC*

ticket kiosk perched up above the road to the right just after the village of Yedidalga. The site itself is not visible from the road, and indeed the Roman theatre is not even visible from the ticket office, lying as it does some 200m further up the hill, approached by a tree-lined path.

Just to the left of the ticket kiosk you can see the **cathedral/basilica** with its beautiful **mosaic and marble floor**. Open to the sky, the mosaics bask under the bleaching sun, their colours fading fast. Among the marble remnants, however, you can still see some magnificent colours: columns in deep brick-red marble with swirls of white, or cool greeny white slabs on the floor.

**Fading mosaics**

The majority of the mosaics are geometric in design, with red, white and dark blue as the predominant colours. Near the centre, the main area of mosaic is chained off in token protection. The centrepiece is a lovely white swan or goose-like bird surrounded by flower motifs, with four small blue dolphins and a pretty multicoloured duck.

At the far end of the basilica a huge tumbled column gives some idea of the size of the whole structure, whose full length must have been close to 200m. The baptistry area was also mosaic, but only with geometric patterns. In the apse itself is a Greek inscription set in an oblong panel, entirely in mosaic. Nearby is a deep well, and scattered all around are thousands of fragments of marble flooring.

The **theatre** lies a few minutes' walk higher up the hill, approached by the tree-lined path. Facing out to sea, it stands on the same site as the theatre of the original Greek city of Soli before it, and had a similar capacity, that is, some 3,500. The town had reached its zenith under the Romans, but was destroyed in the Arab raids of the 7th century. The heavy restoration carried out in the 1960s by the Cyprus Department of Antiquities has somewhat ruined the atmosphere. Everything was reconstructed except the orchestra floor and the platform of the stage buildings, so the seats, rebuilt to diazoma level (i.e. halfway), are all new. The original seats, it is said, were carried off in

**Restored theatre**

the last century to help build the quaysides of Port Said. Local school performances are occasionally held here.

Above the theatre are the scant remains of a **temple to Aphrodite and Isis**, and it was here that the famous, if armless and rather thick-waisted 2nd century BC statue of Aphrodite was laid bare. She is now on display in the Cyprus Museum, Greek Nicosia. Her likeness is often to be seen on wine bottles, stamps and such like, Aphrodite, Goddess of Love, symbol of Cyprus, born from the waves breaking on the shore near Paphos.

**Armless Aphrodite**

> 'Love hath an island,
> And I would be there;
> Love hath an island,
> And nurtureth there
> For men the Delights
> The beguilers of care,
> Cyprus, Love's island;
> And I would be there.'
>
> Euripides, *Bacchai*

Nothing of the original 6th century BC Greek city remains today, and the theatre and basilica are the only visible parts from the Roman city. The rest awaits excavation.

## * LEFKE

### Highlights

Set in one of the lushest and most fertile pockets of the island, Lefke is a pretty and unspoilt rural Turkish town, boasting a new university and three mosques, an unusually large number for northern Cyprus. Its citrus fruits are said to be the juiciest on the island, from the abundance of water. The nearby reservoir is a favourite spot for local picnics.

Lefke is about 5km (3 miles) inland from Soli and the total detour from the coast road to see it need only take about 40 minutes. There are no hotels or restaurants of tourist standard in Lefke.

# Touring Lefke

Following the sign that points inland about 1km east of the Soli ruins, you fork right again at the T-junction that comes 300m later. The approach to the town is heralded by an incongruously stately stretch of dual carriageway with well-tended gardens at the side and a cloaked Atatürk on horseback rearing up as the centrepiece. This ceremonial entry lasts about 500m, and the town proper then begins as the road winds first down and then up again to reach the core of the town. Predominantly Turkish since well before 1974, its 3,800 inhabitants have suffered no displacements or uprooting. Lefke today remains a relaxed and friendly place, sprawling over several hillsides.

**Relaxed town**

The best way to see it is therefore by car; arriving at the centre you come to a fine colonnaded building on the right, then a curious circular stone monument, a **British storehouse** in fact, built to commemorate the coronation of King George VI in 1937. By turning off the main street to the left just opposite this monument, you can wiggle down through a whole maze of narrow lanes lined with picturesque old houses. One lane passes a fine old **aqueduct** some 4m high. Water is everywhere in Lefke, and gurgles in little water channels that run beside the streets.

**Gurgling water**

Returning to the main street, you will see as you begin to drive out of the village, an old mosque in sandy-coloured stone surrounded by colourful gardens, its minaret topped with an aluminium cone. This is Lekfe's main **mosque**, and in its garden lies one of the loveliest Turkish tombs in Cyprus, that of Piri Osman Pasha who died in 1839. Built of white elaborately carved marble in the dervish style with tall turbaned top, its centre is blackened from the smoke of candles, for every time the women of the village ask a favour of the local saint — a husband, a male child, a cure for illness — they leave a lighted candle on the tomb.

**A candle for a wish**

Taking the time to drive a little further afield in Lefke, especially down in the valley, you will cross a wide river bed beside which stands a derelict **small Greek chapel**, raised up next to a grand and excellently maintained house, evidently the seat of the local landowner.

## *  GÜZELYURT (MORPHOU)

### Highlights

The church of Ayias Mamas in the centre of Güzelyurt is, along with Ayios Varnavas near Famagusta, the only one in northern Cyprus to remain open and on view exactly as it was before 1974. There is a certain fascination in seeing the cupboards of the sacristy still bursting with silver chalices and sumptuous priestly robes. The Güzelyurt Museum beside the church has a weird display of stuffed animals, not for the squeamish.

The museum is open daily from 8am until 5pm, and the museum guardian has the key to the church. A visit to both takes about an hour or so.

### Touring Güzelyurt

The Turkish name of Güzelyurt means 'beautiful place'. It is referring less to the town itself than to the surrounding area, where beauty is virtually synonymous with fertility.

Arriving at the large central roundabout of the town, you drive into the little car park in front of the museum, beside the **Ayias Mamas church**. The **museum** opened in 1979 and contains downstairs a remarkable assortment of stuffed animals of the island, including birds, pelicans, reptiles, foxes, rabbits and sheep. Particularly memorable, if somewhat grotesque, are the aberrant lambs, freaks of nature, one with eight legs, one with two heads on its tiny frail body. Upstairs is the archaeological section, with finds from nearby Bronze Age sites, notably Toumba tou Skourou.

**Grotesque exhibits**

Outside, the guardian will, on request, take you across the courtyard of **Ayias Mamas church**, round the edge of what are now the disused 18th century monastic cells. A modern wing of this accommodation was, pre-1974, one of the Bishop of Kyrenia's residences.

Inside the church, it is as if the service had only just finished. The walls and iconostasis (wooden partition separating the nave from the altar area) are resplendent with icons, many of them Venetian, and all of them in excellent condition. Behind the iconostasis, the cupboards are open and still bulging with silver and gilt cups and chalices, and lavish richly coloured robes.

The **tomb of Ayias Mamas** himself is on a side wall beside the entrance, draped in red curtains. In the centre of the sarcophagus is a wooden flap which lifts to reveal two holes where, according to the guardian, 'the Greeks poured oil inside'. Tradition held that the saint's body exuded an oil which cured earache and calmed stormy seas, an oil which was collected from these two holes. Ears, in silver and in wax, still hang beside the tomb, their owners waiting patiently to be healed.

**Earache cure**

Ayias Mamas himself was a popular saint who earned the undying respect of the Cypriot peasantry in the 12th century by refusing to pay his poll tax. He is always shown in icons riding on a lion, because the story goes that when his Byzantine ruler sent for him to be brought before the court and punished, the saint trotted in astride a wild lion and was promptly exempted from his taxes for life. Around 14 churches are dedicated to him throughout the island.

## TOUMBA TOU SKOUROU

### Highlights

The site of this Bronze Age town, like so many Bronze Age settlements, is not of interest to the layman. It is not straightforward to find, and only merits the detour for the real archaeological enthusiast. Its name is known from its finds displayed in the Güzelyurt museum.

There is no guardian so the site is always accessible. The visit will detain you about an hour from the point where you turn off the main road.

## Touring Toumba Tou Skourou

There are no signposts, but leaving Güzelyurt in the direction of Kyrenia, you first cross a wide river bed on a large bridge, followed some 2km (1 mile) later by a small bridge over a much smaller stream bed. Immediately after this bridge, an old tarmac road forks off to the left, leading into the citrus plantations.

**Potsherds among the citrus groves** You then take the first dirt track right, then the first track left to reach a T-junction, at which you turn right again. This track ends in a straw hut behind which, in a clearing, are the ruins as excavated by Harvard University and the Museum of Fine Arts from 1971-74. The area all around is littered with potsherds, and the huge holes left by the giant pithoi (earthenware jars) are in some ways more impressive than the pithoi themselves. Also found on the site was Minoan pottery, Syrian cylinder seals, and some African ostrich eggs. The setting, surrounded by citrus trees a long way from any village, lends a certain charm to the site.

The main road continues east across the plain before climbing up to the village of Kalkanlı. From here a steep descent begins, winding down into the next valley, followed by a shorter climb up to Çamlıbel and Tepebaşı.

# PALEOKASTRO AND AYIA IRINI

As you approach the mound of Tepebaşı a tarmac road leads off to the left towards the bay of Güzelyurt, signposted Akdeniz. This is the road you must take to reach these two sites.

**Intriguing exhibits** Both are remarkable for what was found at them, but since these finds have been removed to museums, there is little of interest left for anyone except the specialist. The 2,000 clay figures from Ayia Irini are one of the most intriguing exhibits on display in the Cyprus Museum of Greek Nicosia. Near Paleokastro, however, is an unusual undergound rock tomb, only recently discovered.

Although Paleokastro lies in an attractive spot on a clifftop overlooking the sea, it is not suitable for swimming or picnicking as it is encompassed by a military camp. Depending on the officer in charge, however, it can sometimes be visited, and you may even be offered a guided tour, followed by tea.

It is 15km (9.5 miles) from the main road to Paleokastro and the total return visit from this point will take about 1½ hours. The military camp is always manned, so you can visit any time in daylight hours. There are no refreshment facilities anywhere along the road.

## Touring Paleokastro

Following the sign to Akdeniz, you begin a drive through heavily militarized countryside. Akdeniz itself, contrary to its name, (which means Mediterranean), is not on the coast but some 2km (1 mile or so) short of it. Its Greek name was Ayia Irini, and this is the name that is well known from the Ayia Irini sanctuary displays in the Cyprus Museum in Greek Nicosia. The sanctuary where these extraordinary terracotta votive figures, all 2,000 of them, were found was not in Ayia Irini village itself, but on a hillock on the coast, at the site which is called Paleokastro.

To reach this you must drive through the semi-deserted village to where the tarmac road stops. At the far edge of the village stands the forlorn shell of a Greek church beside some sheep pens, and at this point you fork to the right along the dirt track, heading towards the sea. The track is well-used because of military traffic and quite straightforward for a saloon car. After some 2km (1 mile or so) you can see the headland on the coast a little to the right, with the military camp on its summit. If you drive right up to the gates, soldiers will soon come running.

**Friendly soldiers**

Don't panic that you are about to be arrested; they are simply delighted to have visitors, a distraction from the routine of the day. Most of the soldiers are on their two year military service stint from the Turkish mainland, rather than native islanders. The Turkish army is highly disciplined, and so as long as you are courteous and decently dressed, there will be no problems, even as an all female party. You leave the car parked outside the gates, and go in on foot.

A soldier will escort you round the temple site of Paleokastro, probably displaying a surprising amount of knowledge. To the layman the site today is no more than a huddle of foundations with one deepish **Well and** well from which a tunnel is said to have led off **tunnel** towards the sea below. Excavated in 1929, the 2,000 votive figures were found round **the temple altar**. Of these, only two were female, a few hermaphrodite and the remainder male, most of them shown wearing conical helmets. They have been dated to 750-500BC.

The coastline here is magnificent, with rocky coves beside the fine sandy sweep of Güzelyurt bay. Currently deserted, there is talk of hotel projects at some unspecified future point.

More interesting to most than the Paleokastro foundations, however, is a nearby **rock tomb**, only discovered in 1988 by Turkish archaeologists. It is thought to belong to a king, as gold and treasure were found inside. The tomb lies about 1km back along the track towards Ayia Irini, some 200m to the left of the road. Although no longer in a military area, it is **Regal** difficult to find without the help of the soldiers since **tomb** it lies underground and is not visible till you are virtually upon it. Built of large well-crafted blocks, the entrance leads down steps into a main chamber with alcoves off it for the sarcophagi of the family members. It is quite likely that more tombs of this sort will be found in the vicinity.

Having returned to the main Kyrenia-Güzelyurt road, you could take the small fork up into the village of Tepebaşı, just for some variation in the route. This and Korucam (to the northwest on the Cape Kormakiti **Maronite** peninsula) were both Maronite Christian villages, and **villages** Tepebaşı was badly damaged in the inter-communal fighting. Many of the village houses near the centre are derelict and crumbling. Higher up the hill, close to the main road, the large domed **modern church** now serves as a hospital and clinic for the military. Korucam remains the main Maronite village on the island, and these Lebanese Christians continue to use their huge church of Ayios Georgios freely: the Turks never had any quarrel with the Maronites.

*

# ÇAMLIBEL (MYRTOU) AND PIGHADES
## Highlights
The short detour through Çamlıbel gives you a chance to see the Monastery of Ayios Panteleimon briefly from the outside, and then soon after, the charming little Bronze Age sanctuary of Pighades, in Cretan-Minoan style, attractively set by itself in the midst of fields.

Ayios Panteleimon cannot be visited as it lies within a military headquarters. The road passes very close by it, so you must content yourself with having a good peer from the car.

Pighades is only 2km outside Çamlıbel, so the total detour including the visit need only take about 40 minutes. There is no site guardian so you can visit any time. It goes without saying that there are no refreshment facilities.

### Touring Çamlıbel
Arriving at Çamlıbel from Güzelyurt, you reach the T-junction with its road block, but fork right towards Lefkoşa rather than left towards Kyrenia. This road takes you almost immediately past the **Ayios Panteleimon monastery** on the right, now within the boundaries of the military camp that seems to **Military** encompass most of Çamlıbel. Ayios Panteleimon was **monastery** the patron saint of doctors. In his pagan youth he had studied medicine at Constantinople, but after his conversion to Christianity he cured the deaf, the blind and the lame by prayer alone. Following his martyrdom, his healing powers were said to have transferred themselves to his silver gilt icon at the monastery. The church was heavily restored in the 1920s, when the monastery was the residence of the Bishop of Kyrenia, and very little of any age or interest remained beyond a few icons of the saint dated 1770. The church was closed in the 1950s and is badly run down.

\*   ## Pighades

This short detour to the small Bronze Age sanctuary is recommended for all but the most hurried. It lies scarcely 2km along the same road that passes Ayios Panteleimon on the way to Nicosia. It is not signposted but as you descend into the plain you should be looking out for a row of cypress trees lining a narrow tarmac road that runs to the right of the main road for about 200m, to reach a cluster of cypress trees set in the middle of fields.

**Cypress trees**

Amongst these trees lies the **Temple** of Pighades (1600-1050BC), with its centrepiece of a small step **pyramid-shaped altar**, some 3m high, built from large stone blocks. It is topped with two stones in the shape of bull's horns, strongly reminiscent of the Creto-Minoan horns of consecration with which it is contemporary. The excavated area has revealed a double courtyard with cisterns, all surprisingly well-constructed for this early date.

**Minoan link?**

The road that continues southeast towards Nicosia across the plain is heavily militarised, each village along the way having been largely transformed into a military camp.

At Yılmazköy (Skylloura) a small road forks to the right through the village towards Gürpinar. Pre-partition maps will show the Prophitis Elias Monastery here on the hillside behind the village, but the area is now a military camp, and the road terminates at the barrier, leaving the monastery tantalisingly in view beyond.

Forking left at Yılmazköy, a road leads off towards Şirinevler, and beyond to the heavily ruined village of Akçiçek with its vandalised church. After Akçiçek, a bad dirt track leads over the mountain range passing through an area of blasting and quarrying, and bringing you eventually, bruised and battered, to Lapta from the rear, or even all the way along the ridge to St Hilarion.

**Bumpy drive**

# LAPTA (LAPITHOS) AND LAMBOUSA

## Highlights

**Superb setting**

Lapta is one of the most picturesque towns in the north of the island, with a superb setting on several mountain terraces overlooking the sea. Formerly Greek, there are three churches in the town, either locked or ruined. Its sister town of Lambousa on the coast below served in Roman times as its port, and some remains of harbour installations like the harbour wall and **fish tanks** are still worth a quick visit. Nearby are two pretty churches which can be seen from the outside.

The two churches at Lambousa are firmly within the confines of a military camp and not visitable. This is a shame as one of them has an early mosaic floor.

A drive around the town of Lapta will take about 30 minutes, as the road network is positively labyrinthine. The visit to the Roman fish tanks at Lambousa will take 1-1½ hours as you have to walk along the coast from the Mare Monte Hotel.

## Touring Lapta and Lambousa

**Fertile terraces**

Lapta lies about halfway between Çamlıbel and Kyrenia, and the turnoff to it is well signposted from the main road. The town is reached after about 2km, but the maze of roads leading up and down and all over the various levels of terraces amount to at least a further 5km (3 miles). These terraces are a natural geological formation, relics of the higher sea levels, and interspersed with huge rocky outcrops, ravines and chasms. One moment you glimpse a church set up above on a cliff edge, and your next view of it is from above surrounded by orchards and still seemingly inaccessible. The best way to get to the highest point of the town is to follow the signs to **Beşpınar Restaurant**, a simple village restaurant which lies right at the top and is very keen to advertise itself. From here you can wind down again by a different route. Water seems to gush in abundance all over Lapta, in one place more like a waterfall than a stream, making it one of the most fertile spots in

**Perennial spring**

Cyprus, famous for its orange and lemon groves. A perennial spring (one of the very few on the island) issues from a rock above the town, at an altitude of some 280m, reached by the road which continues on above the town, beyond the Beşpınar Restaurant.

Under the Romans Lapta was one of the four administrative capitals of the island. It grew still further in the 7th century, when its sister town of Lambousa on the coast was being regularly pillaged by raiding Arabs, like most coastal settlements. When the population moved up the hillside, they carried with them many of the stones from Lambousa to build their new houses at Lapta.

**Ruins of Lambousa**

Today you can still visit the ruins of Lambousa on a headland near the Mare Monte Hotel. From the main Kyrenia road, follow the large sign to the hotel that points off close to the Alsancak turning. Leaving the car at the hotel car park you must walk down the path and steps to the hotel beach. From the beach you walk west, past the bungalows that are ranged to the left of the main hotel, then round the next cove, following the little path right beside the sea. The total time to reach the site from the hotel is 15 minutes at a leisurely pace. This is no longer within the grounds of the hotel, and shepherds are often to be found grazing their sheep in the ruins. It is best therefore to put on something rather more than your swimsuit, to prevent any misunderstandings.

**Advanced fish tanks**

You come first to the **fish tanks** on the headland, the largest of which are the size of a good hotel pool, about 30m by 15m. Guests at the hotel who had stumbled on them during their evening strolls, considered them to be precisely that: the pools of a hotel since pulled down or never finished. They are cut into the rock beside the harbour, and were used by the Roman fishermen to keep their catch alive and therefore fresh for market. Waves splashing over the rock ensured the water was cool and constantly renewed, and intake channels specially positioned to tally with the tides and prevailing winds guaranteed that clean water entered the tanks, while another suitably positioned exit channel guided out the staler warmer water. These tanks are one of the first examples of Roman fish tanks to be found.

Inland from them, on the other side of the path, are the scant remains of Lambousa, sprawling over the headland. The overwhelming impression at first sight is of mounds of rubble everywhere, but this is not so much the work of Arab raiders, as of illicit treasure **Treasure** seekers, digging for their fortunes. Lambousa in fact **diggers** means 'brilliant', a name justified by the quantities of Roman and Byzantine treasure found here, notably the famous early 7th century silver plates depicting the story of David, some of which are still to be seen in the Cyprus Museum. The place was abandoned completely in the 13th century.

The original town was founded by the Greeks in the 12th century BC, but it was the Romans who made it into a major trading centre, establishing a naval base **Roman** and dockyard here. **The Roman harbour wall** is quite **harbour** well-preserved, visible as you walk a little further round the headland. It is still in use with a handful of small fishing boats.

Just 200m beyond the headland to the west, you can see the little churches of Akhiropitos Monastery and Ayios Eulalios, now unfortunately, firmly within a military camp. This section of coastline can also be reached from the main road, by driving down the tarmac fork that runs to the sea directly opposite the sign pointing inland to Alsancak.

The closest church, set in the military exercise ground, is the charming little single domed **Ayios Eulalios**, named after one of Lambousa's bishops. The outer structure dates from the 15th century, but inside it has an early mosaic floor and fine grey marble columns supporting the nave. The **Akhiropitos** **Church in** **Monastery** is within the camp proper and is much **peril** more difficult to see. Its name means 'built without hands' in Greek, from the story, somewhat ironic in the circumstances, that it was transported here intact overnight from Asia Minor to save it from Muslim desecration. It was founded in the 12th century and rebuilt in the 14th century. Disused for some time, the monastery cells were occupied in the 1960s by animals and shepherds. Rising damp had been threatening the buildings for some time before partition, but now the problem requires urgent attention.

# KARAMAN (KARMI)
## Highlights

Curiosity is the main thing that will push you to visit this little mountain village, curiosity to see the only village in northern Cyprus that has been entirely renovated by foreigners, after the new government leased the whole village to the Ministry of Tourism for development. It also boasts a small Bronze Age site and some good restaurants.

Karmi is a 20 minute drive from Kyrenia, and the last part is up a narrow winding road that climbs to the village and stops there. You might time your visit to coincide with lunch or dinner, or even allow an extra hour or so to walk up the mountain path towards St Hilarion Castle, set just above the village.

## Touring Karaman

The 15 km (9.5 miles) of coastline between Alsancak and Kyrenia is now fairly developed, passing a series of hotels, motels and holiday villages. Near Alsancak stands the unfinished 5 star Crystal Cove Hotel whose fate hangs in the balance as long as Asil Nadir's assets remain frozen. Inland from Alsancak, a short detour will bring you to Malatya, a hill village with a fine **Grotto** gorge and permanent waterfall in a grotto on its **diversion** eastern edge.

Some 9km (5.5 miles) west of Kyrenia, just beside the Deniz Kızı Hotel and the Altınkaya Restaurant, is a monument reminiscent of Fascist architecture, its sloping concrete fingers stretching inland towards the mountains. It marks the spot referred to by the Greeks as Invasion Beach, and by the Turks as the point from which the 1974 Turkish Peace Operation was launched. Close by is the National Struggle Museum, with an open air display of guns and tanks, both Greek and Turkish, used in inter-communal fighting from 1955 to the present.

The road inland to Karaman forks off at the sprawling little village of Karaoğlanoğlu, known as **Tiger Bay** by the British, and having a number of good supermarkets and restaurants. It lies just 5km (3 miles) west of Kyrenia. From here the road climbs some 4km (2 miles or so) up into the mountains, passing en route the village of Edremit, where a lot of new houses and villas are being built.

**Tiger Bay**

The road ends at the picture book village of **Karaman**, magnificently set beneath the outcrop of St Hilarion. Formerly a Greek village, it was badly damaged in the fighting, and after partition, the Turkish Cypriot government leased the entire village to the Ministry of Tourism for development. The Ministry of Tourism in turn leased the houses to foreigners for renovation, and the whole place has consequently been rebuilt in old village style, inhabited by expatriates, mainly German and British, most of whom have chosen to retire here. One of the residents retains the key to the church, and opens it to visitors on Sunday mornings. Inside, the church is exactly as it was pre-1974. The three main restaurants are the Crow's Nest, in the style of an English pub, the Duckworth House and the Treasure, set a little below the village in the former Greek school. The neighbouring village of Ilgaz is now also earmarked for similar development. Chronic water shortages have resulted from the development of these villages.

**Show village**

The **Bronze Age cemetery** lies just below Karmi at the entrance to the Duckworth House Restaurant. A sign points along a path which leads to an enclosure boasting a number of tombs which have been dated 1900-1800BC, making them older than the Royal Tombs at Salamis. In the roofed-over Tomb 6 you can just about make out the oldest funerary relief on the island — that of a primitive fertility goddess, heavily weathered.

### ★★★ EAST FROM KYRENIA

## Highlights

The excursions described in this section are among the highpoints of any visit to northern Cyprus and should not be missed by anyone who loves walking and mountain scenery.

**Craggy summits**

The two Crusader castles of Buffavento and Kantara are in spectacular settings perched on craggy summits, and the derelict monasteries of Sourp Magar, Antiphonitis and Panayia Absinthiotissa are nestled in gentle folds deep in the pine forests of the Kyrenia range. As well as the beauty of the settings, the sites themselves are also of great intrinsic interest.

The drive to Buffavento and to the mountain monasteries involves a bit of bumping along forest tracks, but nothing that a saloon car driven slowly

*Castle of Buffavento*

cannot handle. The walk to Kantara and the monasteries is straightforward and gentle, while the climb to Buffavento is on a narrow path with loose rock and takes a good 45 minutes for the young and averagely fit. There are no refreshment facilities at any of these places, and it is best to go equipped with your own food and drink.

**Timings**

The trips to Buffavento and to the mountain monasteries can be done in half days, and whilst it is theoretically possible, if you are feeling energetic, to do all in the same day, it is preferable and more in keeping with the gentle pace of the island to keep the excursions for separate days. The journey along the coast to Kantara certainly requires a full day, as the drive one way takes a good two hours.

## *** BUFFAVENTO

### Highlights

**Dramatic ruin**

An essential outing for all who love heights, castles and adventure. This is the highest of the island's three Crusader fortresses, and the most difficult to reach. Its setting is the most dramatic of any ruin on the entire island. Remember, however, that the final 8km (5 miles) of the approach is a long dirt track, rocky in parts, and that the climb from where the dirt track ends to the summit takes about 45 minutes, often on a loose or steep path, with very little shade.

There is no longer any guardian at the castle, so you can visit any time. The drive from Kyrenia to where the dirt track ends below the castle takes about 45 minutes.

### Touring Buffavento

**An almighty bump**

The distinctive shape of Buffavento's rocky crag dominates the northern coastline, and hovers ever present, beckoning seductively for most of the approach drive. Its outline bulges upwards, as if an unseen hand has struck the brow of the mountain range, making the terrain come up in an almighty bump.

The only road approach is by a dirt track from the east. The really masochistic can, however, make a whole day of it, ascending from Bellapais by donkey on a 12km (7.5 mile) long track, having made arrangements at the village beforehand.

By car, you leave Kyrenia on the Famagusta (Gazimağusa) road, following the coastal strip eastwards for some 10km (6 miles), until you reach the fork left towards Esentepe and the Karpas. You stay on the main Famagusta road as it heads inland and begins to climb up into the mountains, approaching the distinctive **Beşparmak Mountain** to the left of the road, with its five rocky fingers reaching to the sky.

Immediately at the brow of the pass, a stony track (unsignposted at the time of writing) leads off to the right. This is the Buffavento track which you must follow for some 8km (5 miles) as it runs along the ridge of the mountains, giving fine views to the south over the Nicosia plain. The track is rough and stony in parts, especially at the beginning, but a saloon car can manage if driven slowly and carefully, and the surface improves after the first kilometre. From leaving the tarmac, it takes a maximum of 30 minutes to reach the point where the track ends, at an open space with a well under a shady olive tree. During the final 2km you will notice that the land immediately below you belongs to a military camp, and red signs proclaim it as military and forbidden. At one point the shooting range is uncomfortably close, but from your higher vantage point, it is perfectly clear whether or not it is in use. The road you are on is in no way forbidden territory, and as long as you stay on it and never venture downhill, you are perfectly safe.

**Rough track**

**Olive tree**

On emerging from the car at the olive tree, the sheer silence of the place is striking. Above you on the summit are the **distant crenellations** which are your goal, and down below you are aware of the military presence in its incongruous headquarters, the **Ayios Chrysostomos Monastery**.

The monastery itself is not actually visible until you have reached the first level of the castle. From that higher vantage point, you can see the yellow ochre painted walls peeping out from behind the hill which obscures it when viewed from lower down, and a tall old cypress tree stands by its door. According to local tradition, a queen who suffered from leprosy lived apart in the high castle, and her dog, her only companion, caught the disease from her. Slowly, however, he was cured, for he had discovered at the foot of the mountain, a mineral spring with miraculous healing powers. The queen followed him to the spring and was herself cured, whereupon she had the monastery built beside it in gratitude. Today, some of the oldest henna plants on the island are said to grow around the monastery.

**A queen and her dog**

Other traditions have the Empress Helena, mother of Constantine, as founder, but at any rate what remains of the monastery is now largely modern. The double church still has some frescoes of the 11th and 12th centuries which are among the most important on the island. It also retains a magnificent double door, built entirely without nails and set in a frame of carved marble, dated to the 16th century. The monastery is not accessible to visitors these days, but North Cyprus TV recently showed a documentary that revealed the inside of the church. It showed the frescoes whitewashed up to a height of 1 metre 70cm: this was, according to the military, a deliberate act to protect them. The frescoes were restored in 1972 with great skill by the Dumbarton Oaks Byzantine Institute of Harvard University, and their condition under the whitewash is therefore likely to be good. Any faces of apostles that appeared higher than 1 metre 70cm had wallpaper put over their eyes by the soldiers, in accordance with the Muslim belief that the apostles must be blinded. Also out of bounds is the 12th century church, now heavily ruined, lower down the hill below Chrysostomos, on the road to Güngor (Koutsovendis), with its faded fresco of the Lamentation over the Body of Christ.

**White-washed frescoes**

From leaving the car, the steep walk up to the first gateway takes 30 minutes. The path is loose and **rocky**, so appropriate footwear should be worn. Like St Hilarion, the castle is divided into an upper and a lower ward. From the gateway, the climb up to the summit, mainly on steps and often wonderfully vertiginous, takes a further 15-20 minutes. The summit is 955m, and even the Chrysostomos Monastery is at 620m, nearly three times higher than Bellapais. In the last century the ascent was distinctly trickier than it is on today's path, as witness the following description by a Spanish traveller:

**Strenuous climb**

'The peak itself is a rock nearly perpendicular on every side. There was no further trace of a path, so we climbed this natural wall, taking advantage of jutting rocks, projections, holes, anything to which our hands and feet would cling. Sometimes we had to help one another with a stick, or the guide would stop to see where he could get the best foothold, so as to get over the parapet in front of him; and to complete the picture, we had always beside us a horrible precipice.'

Disparaging comments are often made about the paltry nature of the ruins at Buffavento, along with jokes about its name 'buffetted by the wind' meaning that everything on the summit has been blown away. Yet the ascent to Buffavento, because of the terrain and the stupendous location, makes if anything an even deeper impression than the other two Crusader castles, and the wonder is how anything was ever built up here at all.

**Windy summit**

For a time in the early 1970s a guardian was posted

*Sourp Magar monastery*

up here, but he has since abandoned his lonely job. You arrive now at the deserted first section of the castle, entered by a fine **arched gateway**. Inside is a cluster of chambers, one of which is built over a cistern. The **red tiles** used in the arches around the doorways are reminiscent of the Seljuk style of mainland Turkey.

**Vertiginous views**

Right on the summit are the remains of a **chapel** and a few other buildings, but most memorable are the staggering views, often through wisps of cloud, over the coast and back towards Nicosia and the Troodos mountains beyond. Like Hilarion and Kantara, Buffavento was constructed as part of a chain of defence against the Arab raids in Byzantine times. The Byzantine despot king of the island, Isaac Comnenus, fled here to escape the clutches of Richard the Lionheart at the time of the Third Crusade. Isaac's daughter surrendered it and herself to Richard in 1191, and the castle was thereafter fortified by the Lusignan Frankish knights and maintained as a prison called Château du Lion. The Venetians dismantled it fairly thoroughly in the 16th century to deny the islanders any chance of using the inland stronghold in any revolt against them. The Venetians' own interest was restricted to the coast, and they had no desire to maintain costly garrisons in these inland castles.

## ** THE MOUNTAIN MONASTERIES

### Highlights

The ruined monasteries of Sourp Magar, Antiphonitis and Panayia Absinthiotissa all have superb settings deep in the forest of the Kyrenia mountains, and make wonderful spots for peaceful picnics and mountain walks. Sourp Magar has some interesting decorative features, and Antiphonitis still has extensive frescoes.

Much of the driving is on earthy forest tracks, which present no problem for saloon cars unless there has been recent rain. The final 1km of track to all the monasteries is quite steep in gradient, and sometimes deep ruts created by previous rainfall make driving tricky. When this is the case, it is best to walk the final kilometre. There are no refreshment facilities, and should you break down, you are a long way from help.

Sourp Magar and Antiphonitis together form a circuit. The drive from Kyrenia to Sourp Magar is about 55 minutes. From here on to Antiphonitis is about 30 minutes, and from Antiphonitis back to Kyrenia via Esentepe takes a further hour. Including time for walking and full exploration, as well as a picnic, a total of six hours for the excursion should be allowed.

**Timings**

Panayia Absinthiotissa is in a different part of the Kyrenia range and can be approached either on a dirt track from Bellapais leading up and over the pass to Kaynakköy, or from the main Kyrenia — Nicosia road by forking off east at Boğazköy through Asağı Dikmen. Either way takes about an hour from Kyrenia.

## Touring Sourp Magar and Antiphonitis

Setting out from Kyrenia on the Famagusta road as for Buffavento, you again swing inland and begin to climb. Just at the brow of the mountain pass, an unsignposted track leads off to the left (east) towards Beşparmak mountain. If you have visited Buffavento in the morning, and are still feeling robust and ripe for adventure, all you need to do is cross the tarmac road at the brow of the hill and continue eastwards along the crest of the range. In summer it is just possible to complete this monastery circuit in the afternoon and return via Esentepe (Ayios Amvrosios) to Kyrenia in daylight hours.

**Energetic circuit**

For greater leisure though, it is better is to devote the entire day to the mountains and the monasteries, and savour the tranquillity and beauty of the forest. Once you have forked off the main Famagusta road, you may well not encounter another car till you return to tarmac above Esentepe. Both monasteries are utterly abandoned though there is talk of finding a guardian to protect the frescoes at Antiphonitis. On summer weekends the picnic tables at the nearby Alevkaya (Halevga) Forest Station can be full of local families having an outing, but very few visit the monasteries.

The dirt track follows the line of the ridge, hardly ever rising or falling, and passes behind Beşparmak. Because of the absence of gradient, this stretch presents no problem for saloon cars even after rain. After about 8km (5 miles) you will see, if you are looking out for it, the Armenian monastery of Sourp **Forest** Magar peeping out of the forest far below to the left. **drive** To reach it, you must drive a little past it to the Alevkaya Forest Station at a clearing in the wood, from where a smaller track forks downhill to end at the monastery.

Alevkaya is in fact a junction of four roads, and to reach the monastery you must take the only fork that leads downhill to the northwest, slightly back in the direction you came but at a lower level of the mountain. The track, bumpy and rutted in parts, arrives at the monastery after 1km or so.

## Sourp Magar monastery

The atmosphere and superb location, nestling into the crook of the wooded mountains with distant views of the sea, make this an unforgettable spot. Yet as you step down into the terraced courtyard, the desolation that greets you is enough to make you weep. Here in **Desolate** the beauty and silence of the mountains lies this gutted **beauty** carcass, traces of its former splendour apparent at every turn — in the smashed tiles, the neglected citrus trees, and the broken stairways.

Although the last monks left earlier this century, a resident guardian ensured, until 1974, that the place was maintained, and it was even possible for visitors and mountain wayfarers to spend the night in the monks' old rooms. The Armenian community in Nicosia used it as a summer resort, and orphans of the 1895-96 massacres in Turkey were sent here to be educated by the monks. On Sourp Magar's feast day, the first Sunday in May, the place was the scene of much festivity. The monastery used to own 10,000 donums of land covered in carob, olive and pine trees, and crops and vegetables were grown on the terracing below, with the help of an elaborately constructed irrigation system. Now abandoned and unguarded, the monastery has been the victim of wanton vandalism. The monastery church has had its altar hacked to **Smashed** pieces and the Armenian tilework, the only decorative **tiles** ornamentation left here, has been prised off the floor and smashed.

First founded in the year 1000, the current buildings date from the 19th and 20th centuries. The Armenian name Sourp Magar refers to the Egyptian hermit Saint Makarios (309-404), whose Coptic (Egyptian Christian) monastery still stands in the Wadi Natrun between Cairo and Alexandria. This Cypriot monastery too was originally a Coptic one, but was passed to the Armenian church c. 1425.

## Mystery monastery

In the mountains some 15 minutes' walk above the road from the Armenian monastery is an unnamed monastery, heavily ruined, and thought to date from the 12th century. Beside it is a very old and unusual tree tethered with iron ropes. The spot is difficult to find without a local guide.

## Antiphonitis monastery

To reach Antiphonitis, you now return to the Alevkaya crossing and continue east along the ridge, where, after just 200m, you hit a good tarmac road. If you turn right (to the south), this will lead you to the green and fertile Değirmenlik (Greek Kythrea), famous throughout Cypriot history for its abundant water supply, gift of the largest spring on the island. It used to drive 35 flour mills for the inhabitants of Nicosia. Just a short way down this Değirmenlik road you can make a brief detour to the **North Cyprus** **Herbarium** **Herbarium**, a little museum of 800 local plant **detour** specimens pressed or preserved by Dr Deryck Viney, an expatriate resident of Karmi. It is open from 8am until 4pm, and was a project aided by the Forestry Department.

For Antiphonitis however, you turn left and

continue eastwards along the ridge for some 8km (5 miles) until you reach a junction at a bend in the road where the green signpost points to Esentepe downhill on the tarmac road to the left, and straight on to Ormanı Stasyonu (Forest Station) along a dirt track. Follow this picturesque track as it winds and climbs for some 6km (4 miles) until it reaches a signpost beside a huge incongruous electricity pylon. Straight on is unsignposted, as is the smaller track that drops steeply downhill to the left of it, and it is this latter track that will lead you directly down to Antiphonitis,

**Steep descent** nestling below in a fold of the mountain, its red-tiled dome protruding unmistakably from the surrounding green. The steep track is driveable with care in a saloon car, unless there has been recent rainfall, but if you prefer to walk, it will only take 15 minutes.

Architecturally, Antiphonitis is of far greater merit than Sourp Magar, and the lovely **Byzantine church**, centre of the monastery until 1965, dates to the 12th century when it was built by a monk from Asia Minor. The porch and graceful **Gothic loggia** (open arcade) were added in the 15th century under the Lusignans, and inside the derelict shell, its floor now covered in goat droppings, you are staggered to see exquisite frescoes still preserving their colour

**Frescoes** surprisingly well. It was in the wall paintings of such tiny rustic churches, tucked away in remote places, and often financed by private donors, that Cypriot Christian art achieved its own distinctive style, and such frescoes are today their finest legacy.

The **dome** reveals itself, on close examination, not to be a perfect circle, but its disproportionately large size gives it fine acoustics, if you fancy a bit of chanting. Appropriately, the name Antiphonitis means, loosely translated, Christ who Responds. High up in the dome is the lovely deep blue background of the **Christ Pantokrator**, and on the south wall is the unusual Last Judgement scene, both from the 15th

**... and thieves** century. Behind the badly damaged 17th century carved iconostasis and in the southwest corner are the early 12th century frescoes. In recent years two professional attempts have been made, probably by locals under the instruction of international art dealers, to steal sections of these frescoes. These two sections can be identified quite clearly, squares of about half a metre each way, cut into the walls. One of the attempts failed, and the cut-out section crumbled, disintegrating into pieces on the ground. The other is now probably part of a private Byzantine art collection in some distant part of the world. In an attempt to deter this kind of damage, not only to the church itself but also to the Turkish Cypriot image abroad, a group of local people keen to preserve the island's heritage be it Muslim or Christian, are trying to find a guardian to live in the two rooms beside the church. In the meantime they make regular visits to secure the church doors, but as fast as they lock them, they are broken open again by the next set of curious visitors, who, having ventured this far into the mountains to see the church, will do their utmost to get inside.

**Failed attempt**

Today, should you find it locked, it still makes a lovely spot for a picnic, and a little path to the left of the arched entrance leads off to a wide flat rocky platform, the best vantage point for views of the monastery and its disused terracing below.

**Picnic platform**

From Antiphonitis you can, if you are based in Famagusta, take the forest track eastwards from the pylon for 500m to reach a further crossroads at which you continue straight on. Some 300m later there is yet another junction, and from here you can fork to the right, downhill some 6km (4 miles) to reach the village of Tirmen where the tarmac begins again. This dramatic descent can be driven with care in a saloon car, though the villagers are generally rather startled to see visitors approach from the mountain heights.

**Startled villagers**

If you are based in Kyrenia, the more likely return is back down on the northern slope of the mountains towards Esentepe. Returning from this direction, you may spot, about halfway back along the forest track, the forlorn little red dome of a derelict Greek church, overgrown with scrub, with no apparent way to it.

## Apati monastery

This church is in fact all that remains of the 16th century Apati monastery, and as you get closer and pass underneath it, you will notice a poor but driveable track fork off to the left which brings you to within a five minute scramble of it. Set on a wide grassy terrace, it is empty of frescoes and full of goat droppings.

The old village of Esentepe (Ayios Amvrosios), just 15 minutes' drive below Antiphonitis, was noted for its weaving and woodwork. Beside the church in the village square are a couple of restaurants offering simple fare. From here the drive back to Kyrenia takes 45 minutes.

## Touring Panayia Absinthiotissa

This is the least visited of the mountain monasteries, lying as it does on the southern flank of the Kyrenia range and therefore difficult to incorporate into another itinerary. The only maps to mark it are old Greek ones: none of the currently available maps admit to it at all. The monastery itself was originally Byzantine and stands on a platform at a height of 510m (1,700 ft), directly above the village, previously Maronite, of Taşkent (Vouno), now inhabited largely by Turkish refugees from the south. In the centre is a small museum displaying photos of atrocities committed during an attack on the village by Greek Cypriot EOKA fighters in 1963.

**Elusive monastery**

From the top of the village a tarmac road leads north and after about half a kilometre a dirt track forks off to the right near a gravel pit, then right again opposite a water tower. Round the corner another rough track forks up to the **monastery plateau** with the bump of Buffavento lowering to the right. A carefully driven saloon car can manage it all the way to the monastery, though a jeep is preferable. The walk from the tarmac road is in any event only about 15 minutes.

**Well preserved church**

All around the monastery church are numerous outbuildings indicating that quite a prosperous monastic community once flourished here. The church itself is mainly 15th century and is in a good state of repair following some restoration work in the 1960s. Inside are a few heavily defaced frescoes, the main murals having been stolen post-1974, probably by professional black market traders.

## *** ALONG THE COAST TO KANTARA

### Highlights

The 77km (48 miles) drive to Kantara is a magnificent one eastwards along the scenic and as yet unspoilt coast. Unlike the shoreline to the west of Kyrenia, development plans here are in their infancy, and you can still drive for miles without passing any habitation and take your pick of deserted beaches. The castle of Kantara itself makes a fitting climax to the trip, perched dramatically astride the ridge, facing the sea on both sides.

Facilities are limited along this stretch of coastline, with no petrol stations and very few eating places. It is best therefore to make sure you set off from Kyrenia prepared to be self-sufficient.

**Timings** The drive from Kyrenia to Kantara takes about two hours, as the road is slow and winding. There are plans afoot to build a new road all along this northern coastline, and once this is completed, the journey may be as much as halved. At the moment it is best to make Kantara the subject of a day trip, stopping off for a swim or a picnic along the way, and maybe incorporating one of the sights described in the itinerary.

### Touring along the coast to Kantara

There are many places to see along this coastline. None merits a star in its own right, but they are all described here, and you can take your pick of which, if any, you would like to stop at.

### Hazreti Ömer Tekke

Just 4km (2 miles) east of Kyrenia, a green sign points off left towards the coast to 'Hz. Ömer Tekkesi', a delightful little **Ottoman mausoleum** set

**Muslim shrine**

on a headland, where seven Muslim saints are buried. The bumpy track leads down some 2km to the whitewashed domes of the shrine, at the end of a rocky bay. It is open daily from 9am-4pm except Fridays.

## Vrysin

**Beaches**

Leaving the main Famagusta road which heads inland, you continue straight on along the coast, following the signpost to Esentepe. Barely 1km later, after passing a military camp, you come to **Acapulco Beach**, a pretty bay which has been developed into a hotel bungalow and restaurant complex. The open-air self-service beach restaurant here offers reasonable food and the sandy beach is kept clean and has excellent swimming, safe even for the youngest children. The complex also boasts one of the north's few tennis courts. The fee for non-residents gives use of showers, changing rooms and sunbeds.

**Neolithic village by the sea**

On the eastern headland of the bay, just behind the nightclub, is the neolithic site of Vrysin, excavated from 1969-1973 by Glasgow University. Clusters of primitive stone houses were uncovered, thought to have been inhabited between 4000 and 3000BC by neolithic people from Cilicia on the Mediterranean coast of Turkey opposite Cyprus. Among the finds, 250 bone needles and 62,000 fragments of pottery indicated that the Vrysins were weavers and potters rather than fishermen. To the layman today, the site is of little interest, and almost looks more impressive from below when swimming in the sea. The protective fence has fallen over, and visitors are, alas, free to clamber about on the fast crumbling walls.

## Alakati

Soon after Acapulco Beach, you will pass the signs to Lara Beach, a pretty cove of mixed sand and pebbles, a restaurant and a picnic area. After this, there is no village or restaurant along the coast until you reach the area known as Alakati, some 18km (12 miles) from Kyrenia, heralded by a couple of **simple restaurants** set by the roadside a little earlier. The

**Drifting dunes**

potential for this stretch of coastline is enormous, the longest stretch of sandy beach on the northern coast, and in a beautifully wild setting with the Beşparmak mountain as backdrop. The area is also characterised by extensive **sand dunes**, some of which are threatening to encroach on the road. A huge section of this area has been fenced in, having been leased by the Polly Peck ex-multi-millionaire Asil Nadir, a native Turkish Cypriot who invested heavily in the tourist infrastructure of northern Cyprus. Conservationists are concerned at the impending development of Alakati, because of the threat to turtles who currently favour it to come ashore and bury their eggs in the sand. These **loggerhead sea turtles** are now the subject of several active conservationist projects.

**Threatened turtles**

For the moment however, while the fate of all Asil Nadir's projects hangs in the balance, it is still possible to swim at this beach, for the fence does not come across the roads. There are several tracks you can follow to reach the beach. The first leads off at the lowest point of the valley, just past a little bridge with white bollards. This track runs for 1-2km through scattered olive trees to within some 300m of the sea, close to a modern drinking well for animals. The long **sandy beach** is quite magnificent, dominated by the spectacular Beşparmak Mountain. Local folklore regards this five fingered mountain sometimes as the handprint of the Greek hero Dighenis, left behind as he grabbed hold of boulders to toss on to the Arab pirates, sometimes as a testimony to woman's fickleness: the handful of mud that the man threw at the woman when she rejected him. Another track leads off to the small village of Beşparmak at the foot of the mountain, and the energetic can, if they wish, make an assault on its northern face.

**Distinctive mountain**

Peeping round the western headland, the only disfigurement to the landscape is the ugly new electric **power station**, built unconscionably close to the sea, the first one of several planned in northern Cyprus. The north of the island currently gets its electricity from the south, in exchange for water, but this situation will change once the north has completed more power stations.

## Kharcha

Another pretty beach which has the added interest of archaeological ruins, is some 22km (14 miles) from Kyrenia, just 1km west of the sign inland to the village of Karaağaç. It is more suitable for a day trip from Kyrenia than as a stop en route to Kantara, since it takes a good 15 minutes to walk down to the beach from the road. The track to it turns off from the main road beside an old stone farm building. It is too rocky to drive anything more than the first 100m, and then the path descends to the pebbly bay. On the eastern side of the bay is an **old Roman jetty** and section of narrow sunken road. All around are fragments of pottery and crafted stone blocks.

**Roman seaside ruin**

This is the harbour and ancient town of Kharcha, traces of which lie scattered over the hillside to the east of the path. With time and patience, you can still see among the scrub and rocks, cisterns and tombs cut into the rock. One tomb, difficult to find and set underground, still bears a carved face on its lintel.

Along the coast, as you drive further east, you will notice ruined shells of large buildings such as that near Esentepe, just where the fork goes off inland. These are old **storehouses** for carobs and generally date to the 19th century when carobs were exported in large quantities.

**Sticky black gold**

Northern Cyprus is said to produce the best quality carobs in the world, and the pods or locust beans are still exported to the UK as animal fodder. The small beans inside the black runner-bean-like pod are used to make gum, photographic film and a variety of other items. The tree itself has very hard wood and is used for cartwheel hubs and agricultural tools. Altogether, it is a valuable tree, earning its description as 'black gold'. The pods when ripe have a distinctive smell, strong and sickly like squashed black beetle, and the Cypriots make a kind of black treacle from it. The smell was evidently enough to deter fleas, for on St John's Day, 18th July, the peasants would roast carobs and jump over the fire singing 'Fleas, fleas, depart, for the old man is coming with his club'. Carobs are also sometimes known as 'St John's bread'.

Olive trees too, are highly valued, and island superstition says that evil spirits are afraid of them, which means that olive trees are good and safe to take a snooze under. Fig trees on the other hand are disliked, being associated with bad luck and ill health.

## Panayia Pergaminiotissa

Some 2km east of the Esentepe fork, you may notice, if you are looking out for it, a large whitewashed church set in the fields about 1km off the road. A dirt track leads off to it and arrives at the derelict monks' cells, for this was the Monastery of Melandryna. The church lies down in a little dip and has now been incorporated into a local farmer's outbuildings, its floor thick with dung. It is nevertheless impressive, and still has the frame of its wooden iconostasis, with fragments of gold, blue and red paint. The interior is whitewashed, with no frescoes. The unusual buttresses were added in 1731 as a strengthening device.

**Derelict monastery**

## Aphrodision and Galounia

The pretty drive meanders eastwards along the coastline, passing a few modern ruins, the large hulks of buildings which were going to be hotels, bought by Greeks pre-1974, but now abandoned for lack of trade along this lonely shore. Old maps mark an ancient site called Aphrodision here on the coast, just at a kink in the road near the fork to Tatlısu, but nothing remains of it save a few rubble foundations. The same is true of Galounia, 18km (12 miles) further east, at the point where the road heads inland. Both are said to be the capital of the Hittite kingdom of Cyprus in 700BC.

Some 8km (5 miles) beyond the Tatlısu fork you drive through an area where the road is flanked by extensive greenhouses, or long plastic sheds to be more precise. If you look inland at this point you will notice peeping out above the undergrowth about 500m from the road, a **tiny single-domed church** built from

**A church beyond the green-houses**

grey stone. A rough track leads across to it which you can bump along in the car or walk in 10 minutes.

This delicate church, with its tiny ground area in relation to its height, has an almost Armenian feel to it. Scattered all around it are the ruined fragments of what were presumably once its monastery out-buildings. The church entrance has been completely walled up as a measure to preserve the **frescoes** inside. By standing on tiptoe on stone blocks you can still peer inside just enough to make out some traces on the walls.

Still further eastwards the road passes another ruined chapel set beside a group of abandoned houses. Today the chapel is used to pen lambs.

## *** Kantara

At Kaplıca the road forks inland towards Kantara, just after passing another abandoned beach hotel set on its own lovely sandy beach, a good spot for lunch and a swim. You then turn up the **pine-lined street** towards the beacon-like white minaret of the new Rauf Denktash mosque. You can see the castle beckoning from its ridge up above, and the winding drive from here up a narrow twisting road to reach it takes another 30 minutes.

**Twisting climb**

As you reach the summit of the ridge, you enter the little village of Kantara, strongly reminiscent of the Greek summer resorts of the Troodos. There used to be hotels here, but the decline in visitors since 1974 has meant that only one **restaurant**, the Kantara, is left. There are no refreshments at the castle itself, so if you did not bring a picnic, this is your only option.

**Sea on both sides**

A narrow tarmac road now runs a further 4km (2 miles) eastwards along the top of the ridge to end below the castle walls. From here a path, a mixture of steps and earthy ground brings you to the main castle gateway in just five minutes. The relative ease of the approach makes it in some ways less exciting than its two sister castles of Saint Hilarion and Buffavento, and its altitude, at 724m, is also the lowest of the three. It is however unique in having splendid views to the sea on both sides, being sited as it is on the

*Castle of Kantara*

beginning of the island's tapering peninsula, the 'Panhandle', or more correctly, the Karpas, Turkish Kırpaşa. On clear days, especially early in the morning, you can glimpse the distant mountains of mainland Turkey, and even, in winter, the snows of Lebanon, 160km (100 miles) away. The word 'kantara' is Arabic for arch, and accurately describes the sheer rock walls on which the castle is built, making it accessible only from the east. Here, the entrance is guarded by **twin towers**, and steps climb up to the **iron gate** which leads into the castle enclosure.

**Elusive paradise**

Inside, the castle is surprisingly elusive, as the ground plan had to adapt to the rocky contours. Locally the castle was referred to as the House of 101 Rooms, and the popular Muslim belief was that anyone who entered the 101st room would suddenly find themselves in Paradise and unable to go back through the door. Unlike its sister castles, it is not divided into upper and lower wards, but the summit of the mountain rising up in the centre means that the western half of the castle is not visible at all as you enter. Having clambered up to the summit, you will discover paths leading off through the trees and undergrowth to reach a group of **three chambers**, the living quarters, one of which has an emergency exit from the castle. Underneath are two large cisterns still full of water.

Returning along the southern wall, the first building you reach is a **medieval latrine** heralded by a clump of stinging nettles. These are apparently the only plants which can survive the high nitrogen concentration which human excrement leaves in the soil for centuries afterwards. Next to it is a small barracks and more cisterns.

**Panoramic tower**

The best views and photos are to be had from the roof of the **huge northeast tower**, the highest constructed point, and which can be reached with a bit of clambering by those who enjoy heights. This tower is the best preserved of any in the island's three mountain castles, with a fine row of arrow slits in its thick windowless walls.

**Haunting queen**

From the ruined chamber at the very summit, messages were transmitted using a system of flares after dark, first to Buffavento, and thence to Hilarion. At its solitary Gothic window, villagers claimed to see a queen sitting gazing out towards her lost country. She has been there, they say, for the last 500 years, since the castle was abandoned. For 50 odd years in the 19th century, she shared the castle with a hermit called Simeon. The orientation of the castle is towards Famagusta, an hour's horse ride away, and when the Genoese had seized Famagusta from the Lusignans in the 14th century, Kantara was a refuge for many a prisoner who escaped.

**Hunting in style**

The Lusignan lords lived in true feudal style on the island, and on fleeing from Palestine, brought with them their semi-oriental ways and habits. With the fall of Acre in 1291, the last Crusader foothold in the Holy Land was lost, but the knights had grown accustomed to their eastern titles and luxurious lifestyles. Here in the grand quarters of their castles, Princes of Antioch, Tyre and Galilee, Counts of Jaffa, Beirut and Caesaria, pursued the pleasures of the chase, hunting moufflon (mountain goats) with tame leopards. The manes and tails of the horses were dyed red with exotic henna, as were the tails of the hunting hounds. One Count of Jaffa had more than 500 hounds, with a servant tending to each pair.

Also somewhere within this enclosure, 13 Greek monks were sentenced to death by the Lusignan Crusaders who established the Catholic church as the official church of the island. The Greek Orthodox bishops were therefore forced to comply with Catholic beliefs, and when the outspoken ones did not, they were, as a contemporary historian described it, 'condemned to be tied by the feet to the tails of horses and mules, and thus dragged over the rough stones in the market place, or the river bed, until the flesh was torn from their bones, and then burnt'. It is from this time that most of the remoter mountain monasteries date, built far away in the mountains, where the devoted could pursue their faith safe from Catholic interference and persecution.

## Alternative return route

If you are based at Boğaz, a drive of 35 minutes brings you out, via the villages of Turnalar and Yarköy, to the coast at Boğaztepe. If you are at Famagusta or Salamis, the more direct route is via Ardahan and Iskele (Greek Trikomo).

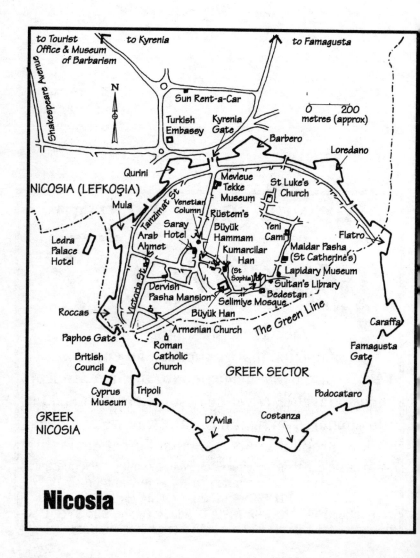

to Tourist Office & Museum of Barbarism

to Kyrenia

to Famagusta

Shakespeare Avenue

N

Sun Rent-a-Car

Turkish Embassy

Kyrenia Gate

Barbero

Loredano

0      200
metres (approx)

Qurini

NICOSIA (LEFKOŞIA)

Mula

Mevleue Tekke Museum

St Luke's Church

Tanzimat St

Venetian Column

Rüstem's

Saray Hotel

Büyük Hammam

Yeni Cami

Flatro

Ledra Palace Hotel

Arab Ahmet

Kumarcilar Han

Maidar Pasha (St Catherine's)

Lapidary Museum

(St Sophia)

Sultan's Library

Dervish Pasha Mansion

Selimiye Mosque

Bedestan

Victoria St

Roccas

Büyük Han

The Green Line

Caraffa

Paphos Gate

Armenian Church

British Council

Roman Catholic Church

GREEK SECTOR

Famagusta Gate

Cyprus Museum

Tripoli

Podocataro

GREEK NICOSIA

D'Avila

Costanza

**Nicosia**

Chapter Four

# Nicosia Region

## ** NICOSIA (LEFKOŞA)
### Highlights

In the featureless Mesaoria Plain that surrounds
Nicosia, there is little to detain the visitor. Nicosia
itself is the worthwhile destination, with a fascinating
collection of Crusader Gothic and Turkish Ottoman
**monuments** set within the old Venetian fortifications.

Anyone who is attracted by things Turkish should
spend a day in Nicosia. Here, within the walls of the
old city, are concentrated the island's major Ottoman
monuments, many of them either still in use, or
renovated as museums. Nicosia is divided into Greek
and Turkish sectors by the euphemistically named
'Green Line', erected by the UN, an ugly barrier built

**Throbbing**
**Turkish**
**heart**

from barbed wire and corrugated iron, cutting across
the heart of the old walled city. The sight of streets
barricaded and houses bisected has a certain eerie
fascination and few will visit Nicosia without taking
a look at the Green Line. The Greeks do not permit
visitors from the north to enter their sector, but those
who have seen Greek Nicosia will be struck by the
difference. Turkish Nicosia has retained the life and
bustle within its walls in a way that Greek Nicosia has
not. The medieval city in the south is a decaying one,
with few ancient monuments, and the bulk of its
buildings, run down and neglected, are inhabited only
by the old and the poor. The heart of Greek Nicosia
has moved out of the walled town into the high rise
suburbs of the modern commercial city.

Turkish Nicosia has had a concerted drive since the

late 1970s to preserve its ancient monuments and to clean up the streets of its old city. The result is a very pleasing intermingling of old and new, for the monuments have, almost without exception, been restored and extremely well-presented for public view,

**Bazaar**  and as you meander from one to the other you pass through colourful shopping and bazaar areas where the ordinary folk of Nicosia are busy going about their everyday business. A stroll around the streets can be broken up by lunch or a drink at the rooftop restaurant of the Saray Hotel, or even by an hour or two relaxing in a renovated Turkish bath.

Accommodation in Nicosia is not of very high quality, and, with no beaches or pretty scenery, there would be no advantage in choosing the city as your base for a holiday in North Cyprus. Summer temperatures in Nicosia and the plain are very high, and it is wise to avoid too much midday walking.

On the new highway funded by the Saudi Arabians, it takes a mere 20 minutes from Kyrenia to Nicosia,

**Timings**  and many people who work in Nicosia commute with ease in half an hour from Kyrenia. Famagusta is a 50 minute drive away. It is therefore possible, especially from a Kyrenia base, to visit the major monuments of Nicosia in a half day, but it will be more leisurely and enjoyable to spend a whole day there. Many of the monuments are closed on Saturdays and Sundays, so choose a weekday for your visit. Parking in the old city is generally straightforward.

## Touring Nicosia
### The city walls

The modern suburbs offer little to the visitor besides good shopping, but as you approach the centre from the north, the one-way system does a wide loop and sweeps round to bring you in through the fine medieval walls at the Kyrenia Gate, which now stands isolated like a traffic island. It looks more like a

**Kyrenia Gate**  bewildered little chapel than a major gateway, as cars and trucks whistle past either side of it, through the two breaches in the walls made by the British in the 1930s. An Arabic inscription above the gate reads: 'O

Muhammad, give these tidings to the Faithful; Victory is from God and triumph is very near. O opener of doors, open for us the best of doors'. In 1878 when the British annexed the island of Cyprus, it was here that the Turkish doorkeeper permitted the British officers to enter the capital. This colourful character, Ali the Cock, as he was known, also made history by living to the age of 121. Today there are plans to open a tourist information office in the upper room of the gate.

**Colourful Ali**

Just outside the gate, near the Atatürk statue, are a couple of **huge iron cannon**, two of several which are to be found displayed here and there in public gardens or on the ramparts. They were British, made in about 1790, from the Woolwich Arsenal, and were used in the Napoleonic wars in Egypt. They found their way here after they were acquired by the Turks.

Nicosia has been a walled city since medieval times, but the walls in their current manifestation are the work of the 16th century Venetians, who were intent on bolstering Cyprus in its role as a major outpost in the Mediterranean to secure their trade routes.

**From catapults to cannon**

The **medieval Crusader walls** before then had been tall with high towers to defend against catapults and arrows, but with the coming of gunpowder, the priority in wall design was to make maximum use of cannon. Hence the Venetian walls are not high, but colossally wide, to allow cannon to be rolled up the ramparts. The population in Venetian times had shrunk, and along with it, the circumference of the Venetian walls shrank from five to three km ( or from about three to two miles). Historical records show that the demolition this entailed, meant that many Gothic buildings were razed and some 80 Crusader churches lost.

**Multi-purpose moat**

The **wide moat** area below the walls was never intended for water, but rather as the open space where, unprotected, the enemy soldiers could be fired at as they approached. In times of peace, the town's dung and rubbish was tossed over the walls as natural fertilizer and good yields of corn were obtained. Today these open spaces serve well as football grounds or public parks, or occasionally, alas, as dumping grounds. From the air they still define the outline of the walls very clearly as you fly over Nicosia. At regular intervals around the circumference of the walls are **11 huge bastions**, six of them now in the Turkish sector, five in the Greek. Of the three fortified gates, the Famagusta Gate and the Paphos Gate, now in the southern Greek sector, were always larger than the northern Kyrenia Gate, reflecting the relative importance of the size of the ports in Venetian times.

**Venetian guile**

The Venetians, belying the beauty and grace of their architecture, were nevertheless unsympathetic rulers. Having built their magnificent fortifications, they proceeded to bleed the islanders of every last drop of revenue, even resorting to such ruses as selling the serfs their own freedom. A Christian abbot at the time spoke for the rueful islanders when he wailed: 'We have escaped from the grasp of the dog (the Lusignan king) to fall into that of the lion' (the Venetian lion of St Mark).

**Hapless queen**

The Venetians acquired the island through diplomatic trickery, manoevring to have the Lusignan James II marry the daughter of a Venetian patrician, Catherine Cornaro. Her husband, and later her son were then poisoned, leaving the hapless queen nominally in charge of the island. In 1489 she was persuaded to retire to Asolo and hand the island over to the Venetian Republic. The Venetian nobles then ruled for the next hundred years, till they lost it to the Turks in 1571.

Unless you are feeling energetic, it is best to drive a quick circuit of the walls on the internal ringroad. Forking east (left) on entering the Kyrenia Gate, you can follow the northern perimeter and pass some older style houses before the road ends at the slogans of the Green Line barricading the street ahead and bisecting the Flatro Bastion. Near the Loredano Bastion on this perimeter street, it is also worth knowing about the

**Cooling ice-creams**

patisserie selling cakes and good ice-cream, invaluable on hot and dusty afternoons. Nicosia has the highest temperatures on the island in summer, topping 100°F.

## * Mevleve Tekke Museum

From the Kyrenia Gate the main road leads you straight on southwards into the heart of the old city, but it is worth stopping first at the Monastery of the Whirling Dervishes, the mystic order of Islam founded by Mevlana, a Persian/Turkish poet of the 13th century. It is the only monastery of its kind on the island, and your eye will be caught by its **low-rise domes** immediately to your left after the roundabout just inside the Kyrenia Gate. Street parking outside has thoughtfully been reserved for visitors to the museum, which is open 8am-1pm and 2-5pm except Saturday and Sunday.

**Mystic monastery**

The early 17th century building was in use as the dervishes' monastery until the 1920s, when Atatürk banned them along with other monastic orders in his determination to make Turkey a secular state. The Turkish Cypriots followed Atatürk's policy and closed the Tekke. The remaining dervishes now have their headquarters in Aleppo, Syria. The Tekke was restored in 1963 and reopened as a museum partly of dervish paraphernalia, and partly of Turkish folk art and crafts, with peasant bridal costumes, traditional knitted socks and embroidery.

The wooden floor is the original one on which the dervishes danced, and at one end stairs lead up to the charming **wooden gallery** where the long-robed musicians played their eerie trance-inducing music. HV Morton described the scene thus:

**Dancing dervishes**

> 'The dancers are dressed in long, high-waisted, pleated gowns that fall to the ground. They wear tall brown felt cones on their heads. Each one, as he begins to turn, stretches his right arm straight up, the palm held upwards to the roof, while the left arm is held stiffly down with the palm towards the earth. The head is slightly inclined to the right shoulder... The dance symbolises the revolution of the spheres, and the hands symbolise the reception of a blessing from above, and its dispensation to the earth below.'

On the walls are some exquisite 18th century Turkish prayer rugs, and old photos, including one of the Pir

Pasha tomb at the mosque in Lefke, described earlier. From one corner, steps lead into the galleried mausoleum of the 16 tombs of the Mevleve shaikhs, row upon row, as if in mirrors endlessly duplicated. Above them are the domes so conspicuous from the street.

## Saray Hotel

Continuing south down the bustling main street, you reach after some 400m the small **Atatürk square**, recognisable by its solitary grey granite column, probably carried from Salamis. In Venetian times it

**Ancient column** carried a lion of St Mark, but the Turks overturned it in the conquest of the island. The British replaced the lion with a copper globe, which is still perched on top. Around the square are the pleasant government offices, built by the British colonial rulers from sand coloured limestone blocks, with elegant arcades and verandahs.

Straight on beyond the square you will see the tall **Saray Hotel**, an ugly modern block whose saving

**Rooftop views** grace is its roof terrace on the 8th floor which provides the best vantage point for views all over Nicosia. Suitable for either lunch or a drink, it is worth taking the time to go up on to its roof, the closest you will come to a detailed aerial view of Nicosia.

From the rooftop, you will be struck by the situation of Nicosia on the flat expanse of the Mesaoria Plain. The only real topography is where the plain is bordered by the **Kyrenia mountain range**, picturesquely forming the northern backdrop. Somewhat less picturesque is the gouging out by the military of the closest south-facing hillside to write the colossal slogan: *Ne Mutlu Türküm Diyene*, How happy is he who can say he is a Turk, addressing or in direct defiance of the Greeks. This slogan is commonly found in the military areas of Turkey.

**Greek/ Turkish contrast** The next thing to strike you from this aerial vantage point is the difference between the Greek and Turkish sectors. To the south, in the area beyond the old walled town, is a distant sea of high-rise blocks, testifying to the prosperity and development of the Greek sector; new building outside the walls in the Turkish sector is much more modest and thinly spread. To the east (right) as you face the twin minarets of the Selimiye mosque, stands the distinctive long four-storey building with white framed window arches, the famous **Ledra Palace Hotel**, now occupied by UNFICYP forces. Beside it is the only authorized checkpoint for crossing between the Greek and Turkish sectors. Ledra was the name of the original ancient settlement on which Nicosia now stands.

It is best to leave the car somewhere near the Saray Hotel and then see Nicosia's monuments on foot. Distances are small and the twin minarets of the Selimiye mosque, always rising above the rooftops, **Homing** act as dependable homing beacons. The major **beacons** monuments are clustered round the Selimiye so a leisurely circuit of them need take no more than two or three hours.

## Circuit on foot

If you start by walking south past the Saray Hotel, you can cross the street to **Rüstem's bookshop**, the largest and best stocked bookshop in northern Cyprus, with a comprehensive selection of foreign books on Cyprus and many other subjects. It is open 8am-1pm and 2-5pm except Sunday, and 8am-1pm on Saturday.

\*
### Büyük Hammam

Forking left immediately after Rüstem's bookshop, you walk down a narrow street, on the right hand side of which, after less than 100m, you will see the Büyük Hammam (Grand Baths), its entrance sunk well below pavement level. This was the level of the street **From** in the 14th century, and the elaborate **entrance portal** **Crusader** carved in stone is now all that survives of the church **church ...** of St George of the Latins, the original incarnation of this building before the Ottomans converted it to a Turkish bath. The sunken level means that the carving on the entrance arch presents itself considerably close for inspection of the intriguing mix of Gothic,

Italianate and Muslim elements.

In 1989 these baths were reopened as functioning establishments, the government having rented the premises to private individuals to run, and it can now be used by locals and tourists alike. Fridays are reserved for women, but all other days are for men

**... to steam bath**

only. If the place happens to be empty, the rules may be bent on this, and you can have it to yourself for an hour or so. This is about the minimum time needed for the process of heating up the body and allowing it to sweat freely in the hot room. Once this stage has been reached you can either give yourself a self-service wash, using the camel hair glove provided, or prostrate yourself on a stone slab for massage and the removal of several top layers of dirt and skin by the vigorous glove-rubbing of the masseur.

In the large domed room you enter from the street, a huge nail high above floor level marks the height reached by the 1330 flood of the River Pedieos, in which 3,000 people drowned.

*Interior of Selimiye mosque, Nicosia*

## * Kumarcılar Han

Continuing past the Büyük Hammam you arrive after some 50m at a little square on the far side of which is the well-restored and neatly presented Kumarcılar Han or Gamblers' Inn, built around 1600. Like all caravanserais, the entrance leads into an open interior courtyard, where the merchants would gather with their donkeys or camels, having arrived bearing their goods for sale. Inside, all the services they required were on hand. Not only accommodation, in the upper rooms of the **arcaded courtyard**, but also stabling for the animals below, along with food and refreshments, blacksmiths and leatherworkers for repairs.

**Merchants' refuge**

An entry fee is charged, yet the inside is disappointingly bare apart from a few carved Roman blocks of stone. Upstairs a couple of the small sleeping rooms have, since 1976, housed the Department of Antiquities.

## ** Büyük Han

A few steps further down the street on the other side of the road is the entrance to the Büyük Han (Great Inn), now in the final stages of restoration, soon to be reopened as a **museum**. This, the largest and most impressive of the caravanserais on the island, was built by the Ottomans in 1572, the year after they seized Cyprus from the Venetians. From the outside, the high windows of the downstairs rooms, even though they were only stables, lend a defensive feel to the building, and indeed their role was partly one of protection for the merchants and their goods from brigands and thieves. The British were not slow to see its possibilities, and used it as Nicosia's Central Prison in colonial times till 1893. Before restoration it served as a builders' yard, cluttered with workshops and decaying machinery.

**Colonial prison**

In the centre of the open courtyard is an octagonal **miniature mosque** with a fountain for pre-prayer ablutions. The other distinctive feature of the han is the tall chimneys, topped with metal pointed cones, as each of the **68 upstairs rooms** had an open fire for the merchants to keep warm at night. Nicosia,

**68 chimneys**

pitilessly hot in summer, exposed as it is to the extremes of the plain, is also fiendishly cold in winter with icy winds.

### *** The hub of Nicosia

After the Büyük Han, follow the narrow street as it kinks to the left, to see rising up before you the imposing facade of the St Sophia Cathedral, now the Selimiye mosque. Beside it on the right is the Bedestan, originally a Gothic church of the 14th century, converted by the Turks to serve as a grain store and clothes market (bedestan means covered market).

**Crusader capital**

This is the **heart of old Nicosia**, and the cluster of five buildings in this immediate area were all originally Christian Crusader structures, converted by the Ottomans in the 16th century to Muslim or secular functions. Nicosia was the **Gothic capital** of the Lusignan kings, and they graced it with magnificent palaces, churches and gardens. Much was destroyed in pillaging through the centuries by Venetians, Genoese, Egyptians and Turks, and earthquakes helped wreak the final havoc.

**Muslim and Christian medley**

The end result, with its medley of Christian and Muslim, cathedrals turned mosques, Greek foundations topped by Turkish roofs, churches reworked as public baths, archbishops' palaces reincarnated as municipal offices, is what makes Nicosia memorable today. As you gaze up at the western front of the cathedral, to the right of the picture are **street barrows** bulging with fruit and vegetables, while to the left are Coke and Fanta Bazaars, offering Southern Fried Chicken complete with white plastic cups and pop music. But this intriguing mix is not the final stage before the city slips into an irredeemable quagmire. It is here to stay; for the air of neglect which hung over this decaying hotch potch just ten years ago has now been superseded by a bustle verging on the efficient, as more streets are cleared of rubbish, and more buildings renovated and maintained.

## ** Selimiye mosque/St Sophia Cathedral

The best place from which to survey the outside of the cathedral is the simple, almost **rustic garden café** reached by walking between the cathedral and the Bedestan. This quiet spot has a superb view of the cathedral's south wall with its **flying buttresses**, and gives the leisure to appreciate the soft mellow golden stone, harmonising against the background of the green cypress trees and the deep blue sky.

French craftsmen began work on the construction of the cathedral in 1209 and, thanks to the stability of its flying buttresses, it still stands today despite the earthquakes of the 15th, 16th and 18th centuries. The roof is flat, a concession to the geography and climate of the Orient, but a curiosity in a building which in all other respects resembles the great Gothic cathedrals of France.

**Nicosia's gem**

The cathedral of St Sophia is, architecturally, the most important monument in Nicosia (Greek or Turkish), with its **superb carving and sculpture** in the triple portalled porch and the colossal high west window. The twin towers were never completed, a fact which made them serve admirably as foundations for the **two tall Ottoman minarets** added by the Turks after 1571. In appearance these additions, labelled incongruous by purists, have been likened to candles with their extinguishers on.

**Working mosque**

Today, as it has done for more than the last 400 years, the cathedral serves as Cyprus' principal mosque, and the greatest celebrations of the two major Muslim festivals (equivalents, if you like, of the Christian Christmas and Easter), are conducted here. Its name change from Aya Sofya mosque only took place in 1954, when the Mufti, the religious head of the Muslims of the island, renamed it the Selimiye mosque in honour of Selim II, the sultan in whose reign Cyprus was conquered by the Turks. Since 1959 the muezzin has been spared the climb up 170 steps to the minaret gallery every day, five times a day, to summon the faithful to prayer, by the introduction of a loudspeaker.

The mosque is open and can be visited any time,

though it is best to avoid the midday prayers on a Friday. During other daily prayer times you can visit but must keep silent. As in all mosques, shoes must be removed at the entrance. No special dress is required, as Turkish Cypriots take a much more relaxed view of bare heads and arms. Inside, the whitewashed interior seems stark, but the **beauty of the proportions** in the high pillared nave is if anything enhanced by the absence of decoration.

**Colourful carpets**

Colour comes in the form of the carpets, predominantly reds and greens, none older than this century, and all of them orientated towards Mecca. This direction is indicated by the highly colourful **mihrab or prayer niche** in the southern wall. The green wooden structure in the centre of the nave is the prayer platform where the prayer leader or imam stands during services, and the **closed lattice gallery** in the north transept is where the women, the few who come to the mosque, are penned. Unlike churches, where the bulk of the congregation tends to be female, worshippers in mosques are almost always men.

**Stripped of decoration**

All Christian symbols and decorations were stripped from the cathedral, inside and out, when the Turks conquered Nicosia in 1570. The Turkish commander, Mustapha Pasha, even had the graves opened and the bones scattered randomly. Some of the tombstones torn up from the cathedral floor now stand in a small room off the southern side of the mosque. Paolo Paruta, Venetian historian and statesman recorded the events thus:

'He destroyed the altars and the images of the saints, and committed other bestial and cruel acts for which he was much blamed even by his own people.'

Venetian historians wrote many such accounts, none of which enhanced the Turks' reputation for clemency. The Ottomans had already taken Syria, Egypt, Rhodes and Constantinople before they turned to Cyprus. With a huge fleet and over 100,000 men, they landed at Limassol which they quickly pillaged and burnt, before moving on to Nicosia, the capital.

**The siege of Nicosia**

Hearing of the advance, the terrified government gathered the men, women and children within the walls. The Venetian governor at the time was one Nicolo Dandolo, 'a man whose ineptitude was so apparent, his supineness so glaring that it verged on treachery', as one historian wrote. The odds were hopeless. Within the walls were 76,000, of whom only 11,000 were capable of fighting. The strength of the walls was such, however, that the siege lasted 48 days before the city fell. In the market place of Nicosia a funeral pyre was made of the old, the infirm and the ugly, and the acrid smoke filled the city for days. When the Ottoman ships returned to Constantinople, they were bulging with as many slaves and as much gold and jewels as they had been able to cram aboard. 20,000 Turkish soldiers were left behind to settle on the island, and more were subsequently encouraged to emigrate from the mainland.

**Supine governor**

The Turks retained control of the island for the next three centuries, but despite much mismanagement, along with nature's contributions of famine, drought, and plague, there were some important developments. The Greeks were given more autonomy than they had ever enjoyed under any previous ruler. The feudal system imposed under the Lusignans and perpetuated under the Venetians, in which the peasants were forced to work without pay for several days a week, was abolished. The everyday life of Cypriots was also made easier by such foundations as water fountains distributed all over the cities for the first time. A few are still in use today. The Turks rarely went in for building fancy, self-glorifying edifices like Roman triumphal arches or Egyptian pyramids. Their legacy lay in social welfare buildings, like aqueducts, mosques, tekkes, caravanserais, schools, libraries and baths.

**Three centuries of Turkish rule**

No attempt was made to impose Islam on the native population. The Latin Catholic priests were expelled, and the Greek Orthodox Church was restored. The Greeks in fact tore down many Latin Gothic churches and the remainder were turned into mosques or

**Tax collector**

**Political head**

stables. The Turks gave the Orthodox Archbishop the responsibility for collecting taxes from both Greek and Turkish elements of the population, and in return, the Church was itself exempt from any tax it collected in excess of the tribute specified. It was from this practice that the habit was established of the Archbishop being regarded as the de facto head of the Greek Cypriots, a role which was frequently misused from then until Archbishop Makarios, under whom the Cypriot Church overreached itself for the last time. William Turner, a British diplomat staying on the island in 1815 wrote:

> 'In short, these Greek priests, everywhere the vilest miscreants in human nature, are worse than usual in Cyprus, from the power they possess. They strip the poor ignorant superstitious peasant of his last para, and when he is on his deathbed, make him leave his all to their convent, promising that masses shall be said for his soul.'

## * The Bedestan

The now semi-ruined Bedestan was originally two churches, and served as the Greek Orthodox cathedral during Venetian times. The Turks later put it to the twin uses of grain store and clothes market. Its interior is badly damaged, with repaired pillars supporting arches. It is empty save for a few **medieval Muslim tombstones**. The guardian, who is usually to be found in the vicinity, keeps the key for this, for the Sultan's Library, and for the Lapidary Museum.

**Gargling gargoyles**

The Bedestan's most noteworthy feature is its **entrance portal**, elaborately carved. Especially fine are the gargoyles, their mouths grotesquely shaped to act as spouts for the rain gutters. The gargling noise of the water bubbling through their throats has given us our word 'to gargle'. The British in 1879 put forward a plan to convert the Bedestan into an Anglican church, but the Muslim community rejected this as provocatively close to their mosque.

## The Sultan's Library

Skirting the south wall of the cathedral, past the garden café, you walk under the arch of one of the massive buttresses to reach the Sultan's Library just at the back of the cathedral. It was named after Sultan Mahmoud, who had it built in the early 19th century. Immediately before it to the right, the fine old two-storeyed crenellated building with Gothic windows was once the **Chapter House**. Upstairs it is now the Marmara Pansiyon, while downstairs is a carpentry workshop of the Antiquities and Museums Department.

**Wall to wall books**

The guardian opens up the tall doors of the library that lead into the single square room covered from floor to ceiling with bookcases. The books themselves are in Turkish, Arabic and Persian, and a few are on display in showcases. The gilded ceiling rail under the little domed roof has Koranic inscriptions.

From the library, you can study the back end of the cathedral/mosque, with its elaborate doorway, now closed. In the mixture of elements so typical of Nicosia, Greek white marble columns flank the doorway, with pictures of green cypress trees either side of Arabic texts from the Koran.

**\*\***

## Lapidary Museum

The guardian of the Bedestan will now, if you ask him, open the wooden doors to this remarkable museum just a few metres further east, using the **largest key** you are ever likely to see, reaching from

**Giant key**

his elbow to his wrist. Inside this Venetian nobleman's house, the English colonial rulers, with their love of antiquities, gathered together fragments of stonework from Nicosia's ancient palaces and churches.

The upstairs wooden gallery has some splendidly **carved pulpits** and lecterns, along with some magnificent wooden doorways of mosques and churches. In the open courtyard below, the white **stonework fragments** are alive with gargoyles, their expressions both revolting and hilarious. Each face is different, though they are always male. Like latter day

**Spitting images**
Spitting Images, these gargoyles gave the artists the chance to ridicule the figures of their world; the priests, their fellow workers, or petty officials. The practice still continues, viz the modern gargoyle wearing spectacles, carved in summer 1989 on to the porch of Chichester Cathedral in Sussex, England, a perfect likeness of the retired dean.

A fine lintel in the courtyard has been thoughtfully made into a bench, and nearby are Crusader shields and prancing lions. Most striking of all, however, is the splendid Gothic stone **tracery window** in **Last flamboyant relic** 'Flamboyant' style, flanked with a face on either side, which forms the centrepiece of the back courtyard. This is the last surviving relic of the Lusignan palace which once stood on the site of the government offices beside the Venetian column in Atatürk square, near the Saray Hotel. The Turks adapted it for their use and called it the Serail or Palace. A traveller in 1845 described it as 'a poor crumbling lumber chest, with hanging doors, rotten floors, and paper window panes', and so when it fell into total disuse, only the Crusader stonework remained intact.

## Fountains and the Archbishopric Palace

Skirting round the cathedral from the northern side, you will notice to the right a small fountain set in a pointed arch. Many of these **Ottoman fountains** can be seen on street corners all over old Nicosia, and two of them are even still in use. That on Tanzimat Street is especially fine.

Just beyond the fountain, a little way up a side street to the right (north) is the **Latin Archbishopric Palace**, formerly a Muslim school, now the **Elegant residence** headquarters of the Organization of Turkish Municipalities of Cyprus. You can still stroll into its neat **cloistered courtyard**, with two elegant outside staircases leading to the upstairs section which was rebuilt in the Ottoman style after the Turkish conquest, to serve as the residence of the Chief Judge.

## \* Haidar Pasha mosque/St Catherine's Church

Returning to the Lapidary Museum you can follow the road that runs to the north along its left hand wall to bring you, after 100m or so, to the Haidar Pasha Mosque, originally St Catherine's Church, instantly recognisable by the Gothic windows and the tall **Vertical** minaret. The stone is the same sandy limestone as that **lines** used in all these Gothic buildings, and the distinctive **mellow colour** helps it to stand out from the later surrounding buildings. After the cathedral, this is the most important of Nicosia's mosque/churches, **unusual architecturally** because of the many tall arcaded windows requiring extra buttresses to strengthen the walls. The style is called Gothic **Extra** Flamboyant and it dates to the late 14th century. The **buttresses** building has at last undergone internal restoration, UNESCO funding for the project having been withdrawn post-1974, and now serves as an exquisite private art gallery. At one stage it was used as a Marriage Registration office.

## Yeni Cami and St Luke's

Those whose appetite for mosque/churches is not yet sated can walk on for a further 20 minute circuit to see the Yeni Cami and St Luke's.

Heavily ruined, with only a staircase and one fragmented arch remaining, the Yeni Cami was once **Treasure** a 14th century church. It owes its dilapidated state to **search** one of the more demented Turkish governors, who tore it down in the 18th century in a frantic search for buried treasure. The name means New Mosque, given to it because the temporary mosque built afterwards on its site had to be built almost from scratch.

St Luke's stands in the middle of an open playground area and is now kept locked, though a notice on its door describes it as the Popular Crafts Society. Unlike the other churches described, it was never a converted mosque, since it was in fact built under Turkish rule, like many other churches, in the 18th century. In style it is Byzantine, with a **bell tower**.

## * Towards the Armenian Church and the Green Line

Returning to the Bedestan, a more interesting diversion can be made to see the old quarter in the western area of walled Nicosia, where the best examples of Ottoman and British **colonial houses** are to be found. Retracing your steps up the bustling street west from the Bedestan, instead of forking right to pass the entrance of the Büyük Han, you keep heading west, straight on, passing through a pedestrian precinct shopping area selling jeans and all sorts of clothes and shoes.

Keeping on this westward course, you will come after some 300 or 400m to an open area with a children's playground on your left, across which, in the distance, behind a military playground and fence, rises the bell tower of the lovely **Armenian Church**. This is unfortunately about the best view you will get of it, for it is now a military headquarters, and when approached from the street, is entirely shielded behind high walls and gates.

**Military church**

It was originally a **Benedictine convent** and the walls conceal an unfinished Gothic cloister. The Abbess in the 14th century was involved, so the story goes, in an intrigue to murder the Regent, the Prince of Tyre, and was accused of sheltering the assassin. Soldiers broke down the gates and threatened the holy sisters with death and dishonour. The Abbess appealed to the Papal Legate for protection, and she and her nuns were finally spared.

**Intrigue at the abbey**

The convent was much altered and repaired over the centuries, and was in use as a **salt store** when the Turks gave it to the Armenians. The area here around the Paphos Gate had long been the Armenian quarter.

Behind the Armenian Church and just on the Greek side of the Green Line is the **Roman Catholic Church**, recognizable by its distinctive spire. A walk down this street is to be recommended for the succession of lovely houses it offers. Aptly named Victoria Street, the houses were built from the time of the British occupation in 1878, and their distinctive feature is the curved **ironwork balcony** above their

**Colonial houses**

huge doorways. No. 73 Victoria Street is a good example, built in 1923. Continuing south, you can walk down the street towards the Green Line until you notice the soldier twitching his rifle, at which point it is best to turn back.

The **Green Line** is in fact a somewhat euphemistic description of the extremely physical barrier of bricks, barbed wire and corrugated iron that divides the old

**Barrier of bric-à-brac**

city into two roughly equal halves, abruptly bisecting streets that used to run straight on, rudely separating houses that were once neighbours. In the suburbs of Nicosia, it is extended by the **Red Line**, becoming the **Attila Line** once out of the city. Within the old city, the Green Line has now become something of a tourist attraction, with German tour groups especially seeing in it shades of the Berlin Wall, and being conducted to view it from several places on the north.

## * Dervish Pasha Mansion

Facing out over the children's playground towards the Armenian Church stands the newly renovated Dervish Pasha Mansion, opened in 1988 as an **Ethnographic Museum**. Dervish Pasha himself was the editor of a newspaper called Zaman (Time), the first Turkish paper in Cyprus, in 1891. Immaculately presented

**Attractive museum**

with whitewashed walls and blue woodwork and rafters, the museum is laid out in a room by room recreation of an early 19th century mansion. Downstairs are the service rooms: kitchens, stores, with displays of cooking utensils and agricultural implements, while upstairs are the living quarters, furnished with relics of a lavish lifestyle: embroidered

**Ottoman lifestyle**

bathtowels, exquisitely delicate purses, fine old carpets, and sumptuous clothing.

In the open courtyard are the baths and wash rooms, and in a corner, a prettily laid out **refreshments area** offers tea and soft drinks.

## Arab Ahmet mosque

Forking north (right) up Victoria Street (Salahı Sevket Sokağı) after the Dervish Pasha Mansion, you will arrive at the Arab Ahmet mosque at the corner of the next major road intersection, set on the left in a lush graveyard. What seem at first glance to be Roman columns in the neat gardens are in fact **tall tombstones** of various eminent pashas, the fine white marble orginally from Beirut. The mosque is a typical example of 19th century Ottoman, restored in 1955, and the spot is attractive more for its trees and graveyard than for the building itself. Inside are the usual whitewashed walls with medallions near the dome bearing the names in Arabic of Abu Bakr, Umar, Uthman, Ali, Hussein and Hassan, the first caliphs of Islam. The pulpit is, as so often, painted green, the colour of Islam, and beside it is the mihrab, the prayer niche which indicates the direction of Mecca, so that the faithful can orientate themselves correctly during prayer. The crass modern carpets conceal the tombstones of some Frankish knights, reused in the floor paving as conveniently large slabs. The mosque guardian will pull back the carpets if you ask to see.

**Pretty gardens**

*Arab Ahmet mosque, Nicosia*

## Exit from the walled city

By car, the one way system encourages you to leave from the Saray Hotel area in a westerly direction towards the walls and then north along Tanzimat Street, where many older style private houses can be seen. Some of these, exposed as they are to the Ledra Palace Hotel directly across from the Venetian ramparts, were targets for the EOKA terrorists, and many of the houses still bear the bullet holes. Also on this street, the old women, enjoying the chance to meet neighbours and gossip, still collect water from the old **octagonal Ottoman fountain** with its fine brass taps set in elaborate panels.

**Elegant fountain**

Heading north inside the walls, the Mula Bastion is now a disused military area, and at the Qurini Bastion, the large white building is the **President's residence**. Before partition, it was designated the Vice President's Palace, and Rauf Denktash still has his official residence here.

**President's residence**

## The suburbs

As you enter Nicosia from the north, the main road crosses a bridge over a **river bed**, almost invariably dry. No river in Cyprus flows all the year round, and the water courses are highly seasonal, full and rushing after a heavy downpour, dwindling to a trickle shortly after. When Nicosia was founded in the 4th century BC, it lay on the banks of the Pedieos (Turkish Kanlı) River, and the plain all around was thickly forested.

After the river bridge, a fork can be taken to the right at the traffic lights, to follow a road which runs more or less parallel to the main street. Now Mehmet Akif Caddesi, this was called **Shakespeare Avenue** and is still commonly referred to as such by the foreign community.

Some 500m south is the **Tourism Office** for Nicosia, not really worth a visit, as the assistants will simply hand out the same glossy pamphlets that you have probably already picked up elsewhere.

Opposite the Tourist Office is a sign startlingly announcing the Museum of Barbarism. It is the house where the family of a Turkish Cypriot major was

**Museum of Barbarism** murdered by EOKA fighters in 1963. With its chilling display of blood and brain splattered on walls and ceilings, the museum is not for the squeamish.

## ACROSS THE MESAORIA PLAIN

East from Nicosia, the character of the landscape changes as you enter the vast expanse of the Mesaoria Plain. It is not an area worth visiting in itself, but simply has to be crossed on the way to what in most cases will be Famagusta or Salamis. Some background is provided here to help relieve the monotony of the journey. Fertile but now near treeless, the Mesaoria was once thickly forested. Hunting wild animals was **Death of a** the great sport of the early rulers, and whole retinues **forest** of nobles, barons and princes would go into the forest for anything up to a month at a time, living in tents. One account written in 1336 described how the party took with it 24 leopards and 300 hawks to aid in the sport. By the 16th century, many species verged on extinction. The huge forests were gradually cut down for domestic fuel, but also for smelting in the copper furnaces throughout the ages. The abundance and ease of obtaining this fuel enabled Cypriot craftsmen to attain a high standard of metallurgy, and Alexander the Great is said to have had a Cypriot sword. Great **Metallurgy** expanses were also cleared for crop growing. The plain owed its fertility to the alluvial deposit brought down from the mountains in heavy winter rains, like the fertility bestowed on the banks of the Nile in flood. As the climate changed over the centuries, less and less rainfall occurred and the area around Nicosia became a semi-desert like plain.

From Kyrenia, the drive to Famagusta is 73km (46 miles) and takes about an hour and 10 minutes. From Nicosia it is 61km (38 miles) and takes about 50 minutes.

### Touring the Mesaoria Plain

The longer (one hour and 15 minutes) but more interesting route than by the main highway, is via **Ercan**, a former military airport (previously called

Tymbou). It was constructed by the British in World War II, and has now been transformed into a small but quite slick passenger terminal for all non-military flights that connect to the Turkish mainland. Turkish Airlines run flights into Ercan, not only from Istanbul and Izmir, but also from Ankara, Adana and Antalya. Its location is convenient, for the transfer time to both Kyrenia and Famagusta is only about 40 minutes.

8km (5 miles) west of Ercan, at **Gaziköy**, is the only antiquity along this route, an **Ottoman aqueduct**. It runs close beside the left of the road, quite well-preserved for a long stretch, beginning about 1km before Gaziköy. One of the major legacies of the Ottomans was to transform the water distribution on the island by building several such aqueducts, and the water was sent, not just to wealthy rulers' houses, as had been the case under previous occupations, but also to public fountains in the cities and towns, introducing a higher standard of hygiene and cleanliness than had been possible before.

**Legacy of aqueducts**

The villages you pass along this route have interesting old rural style houses, and lifestyles here have remained largely unchanged since the 18th and 19th centuries. The streets also have more than their fair share of mud. After rain, the whole area is very liable to flooding, with roads and fields becoming indistinguishable in sheets of water. Rain in Cyprus can often be violent, and it is not unusual, any time from mid-October to mid-March, for two or three inches to fall in a day. It is mercifully brief, though, and the day after is quite likely to be bright and sunny.

**Rural houses**

Further east, Pasaköy is, like so many villages in the vicinity of the Attila Line, a bit like a military garrison. Though the forest of military barriers is a little daunting at first, you are in fact never stopped as a tourist vehicle. South of Pasaköy near the village of Erdenli (Greek Tremetousha), you may feel tempted to visit **Ayios Spiridon**, the monastery marked on some old maps. It is however heavily guarded, due to its proximity to the Attila Line, and no attempt should be made to approach it. One of the oldest and largest

**Heavily guarded icons**

monasteries on the island, Ayios Spiridon was also the place where icons were sent for restoration from all over the island. As a result, it has the largest collection of valuable icons in northern Cyprus. Though not on view to visitors, independent archaeological authorities have been allowed in to see them since 1975 and have confirmed they are all safe and neatly catalogued.

The road on to Famagusta forks north through Turunçlu. If you are continuing to Salamis rather than Famagusta, be careful not to miss the fork left near Mutluyaka to save yourself the unnecessary and

**Industrial fringe**

unsightly detour through the **industrial outskirts** of Famagusta. The traffic along this road is, by northern Cypriot standards, very busy, with many lorries and goods vehicles heading for the commercial free port of Famagusta.

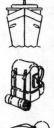

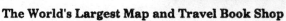

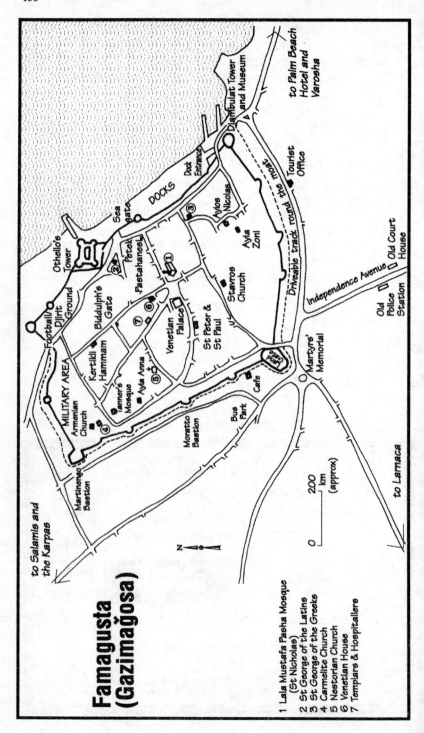

# Famagusta (Gazimağosa)

to Salamis and the Karpas

to Palm Beach Hotel and Varosha

Djambulat Tower and Museum

DOCKS

Dock Entrance

Tourist Office

Driveable track round the moat

Sea gate

Othello's Tower

Martinengo Bastion

MILITARY AREA

Football/ Djirit Ground

Armenian Church

Kertikli Hammam

Biddulph's Gate

Petek Pastahanesi

Ayios Nicolas

Ayia Zoni

Stavros Church

Tanner's Mosque

Ayia Anna

Venetian Palace

St Peter & St Paul

Moratto Bastion

Bus Park

Cafe

Martyrs' Memorial

Old Police Station

Old Court House

Independence Avenue

to Larnaca

N

0    200    km (approx)

1 Lala Mustafa Pasha Mosque (St Nicholas)
2 St George of the Latins
3 St George of the Greeks
4 Carmelite Church
5 Nestorian Church
6 Venetian House
7 Templars & Hospitallers

## Chapter Five

# Famagusta Region

### Highlights

**Finest beaches**

If beaches are your priority, then the Famagusta region is for you. The immense sweep of Famagusta Bay is one of the finest stretches of sand anywhere in the Mediterranean. The hotels of the region are almost entirely along this bay and have excellent beaches and water sport facilities. For sightseeing, the major classical site of the island, Salamis, is on your doorstep, Kantara Castle is close by and you are well-placed to explore the Karpas peninsula.

As a base for a holiday on the island, the Famagusta region is more limited than Kyrenia. Most meals will probably be taken in the hotel, since eating elsewhere becomes an excursion in itself, unless you are staying in Boğaz. Shopping is a lot less sophisticated. Visits to the major sights of the Kyrenia area, like Bellapais and St Hilarion become quite lengthy trips, and visits even further west to places like Vouni and Soli become impracticable. The flat landscapes inland from the bay can also become a bit monotonous.

**Timings**

From Famagusta the drive to Kyrenia takes about one hour and 10 minutes, and to Nicosia about 50 minutes. Ercan airport is 40 minutes away. From the walled town of old Famagusta it takes 10-15 minutes to drive to Salamis.

## ** FAMAGUSTA (GAZIMAĞOSA)

### Highlights

The old town of Famagusta boasts some of the most **superb medieval architecture** in the Middle East, and no less a figure than Leonardo da Vinci is thought to have been involved in the design of its **colossal Venetian fortifications**. Within the walls an intriguing range of monuments, mainly churches, can still be visited.

**Startling contrasts**

Famagusta (Turkish Gazimağosa) today is a fascinating hotchpotch, perpetually startling in its incongruities and juxtapositions. Here a Leeds steam locomotive stands in front of the Turkish Police Station against the backdrop of skyscraper shells in decaying Greek Varosha. There a Crusader church appears in the garb of a municipal library, while another serves as a café. One tower built by Venetians holds a museum to Ottoman military might, and another holds the ghost of Shakespeare's Othello. In the main square, the French Gothic cathedral, topped with a misshapen minaret, faces out at the façade of a Venetian palace supported by Greek marble columns from Salamis. Next door, the Faisal Islamic Bank, once an Ottoman school, looks across at a Turkish bath, now converted to a trendy bar and restaurant. Today's Turkish inhabitants have blended the city's relics so casually with their own daily needs, that the preservation of these monuments is almost synonymous with the routine maintenance of their public buildings and offices.

**Quiet walled town**

It is by no means a beautiful city. The modern town has the extensive industrial sprawl that belongs to a bustling port. The old walled town in the centre, scruffy and medieval, and still with large areas of bombsite wasteland, seems sleepy and quiet in comparison.

Famagusta has little of the sophistication of Kyrenia or Nicosia. Apart from the 5 star Palm Beach, there are no hotels of tourist standard in the town. These all lie further north near Salamis. Good restaurants are few and far between, especially inside the walls. The surrounding landscape is flat and featureless, and the busy commercial port means that traffic is heavy, with many noisy goods vehicles.

One full day should ideally be devoted to Famagusta, to give yourself time to stroll in the

**Planning your itinerary** streets of the old walled town seeking out the early churches and Venetian buildings, and to explore the walls and bastions fully. These are really Famagusta's most remarkable feature today, and if you are limited to just a couple of hours, the essentials could be reduced to a drive round the walls from the outside, noting especially the Land Gate with its drawbridge, and the Martinengo Bastion; a walk round Othello's Tower; and a walk round the St Nicholas Cathedral/Lala Pasha Mosque in the main square. The ghost town of Varosha, the modern Greek suburb which is now a sealed-off no man's land, also holds an eerie fascination and is worth a quick look from the car.

## *** The walls of old Famagusta

Any visit today would best begin with a tour of the walls. Originally Lusignan Crusader, these walls were redesigned and strengthened by the Venetians, making the square towers round and generally adapting them for cannon warfare rather than the outmoded bow and arrow. The result was to make Famagusta one of the most impressive walled cities in the Middle East. To appreciate them properly it is best to drive around the moat gully, viewing them from directly below.

**The mighty Martinengo** As you enter the bustle of modern Famagusta from the direction of Salamis, you arrive at a roundabout with a sign to Geçithavaalanı. At the roundabout, you take the left exit, west towards the sea, and this road will bring you over a little hump to the northern edge of the walls at the mighty **Martinengo Bastion**. Squat and muscly rather than tall and towering, these Venetian ramparts are not visible from the modern town until you are nearly upon them. Their height, some 15m, is less than twice their width, often 8m. At the turn of the century, before the industrial development had burgeoned, the imposing outline of the cathedral within the walls could be seen from a great distance as you approached. The soft brown limestone that was quarried to create the moat was then used to construct the walls, an immense task, which must have taken decades. Fifty years is the

**50-year task** usual estimate. Leonardo da Vinci is recorded as visiting Cyprus in 1481, and is thought to have advised his fellow countrymen on the design.

A slow drive around the moat takes just ten minutes, and you can get on to the track either at the point where the road enters the walls from the north, or from beside the Djamboulat Bastion on the south. **Circuit of the moat** The circuit can of course also be done on foot, and in the winter months makes a pleasant stroll of about an hour. North of the Land Gate you pass by a pretty café offering simple refreshments, set down in the moat. Apart from this, the moat is invariably deserted. In summer, when the heat is trapped in the airless gully, all but the most hardy would be best advised to save their energy for the walk within the walls, in itself more than sufficiently sapping. In many places around the moat, especially between the Land Gate and the Djambulat Tower, you can still find **old cannon balls** and other bits of metalwork left over from the Turkish bombardment. Iron was expensive, and whenever possible, the bravest soldiers would sneak into the moat at night to retrieve the cannon balls for reuse.

As for the ramparts themselves, you can still walk along the top of them with ease between the Djambulat and the Land Gate. In the 1930's, the British colonialists, ever amused by games, engineered **Golf on the ramparts** a **9-hole golf course** on top of the ramparts, on which 'the accuracy of direction' more than made up for 'the comparative shortness of the holes'. If you are prepared to be agile, you can also walk a little way from the Land Gate towards the Martinengo Bastion, though you will certainly be stopped soon after the Moratto Bastion as the area becomes military. A large chunk of northern walled Famagusta is now a military zone and consequently out of bounds, which is unfortunate since four of the city's 15 standing churches are still there.

The Martinengo Bastion also falls within this military area, and as a result, the fine craftsmanship of this, the most powerful of the 15 bastions, can only be viewed from the outside. It is named after a

Venetian commander who was sent to Cyprus to relieve the Turkish siege, but who died at sea before arriving. His remains are buried here.

The **Land Gate** is certainly the most impressive of the bastions, with its arched stone **19th century bridge** spanning the moat, on which traffic, one-way only, is allowed to enter. Today it also houses the Post Office, and beside it is a colossal ramp leading up on to the walls, used for rolling up the cannon. It takes a full 15 minutes to explore its labyrinth of rooms, dungeons, steps, ramps and arches, and its darker recesses have latterly been serving as impromptu latrines, so watch your step. Here and there in the ceiling, chimney holes can be seen, essential to let out the smoke that billowed up every time the cannon were fired. The cannon used by both the Venetians and the Turks during the siege of Famagusta in 1571 were more powerful than any ever used before in any other country.

**The huge Land Gate**

It was the sheer power of Famagusta's walls that enabled it to hold out for ten months against the Ottoman Turks. Nicosia had fallen in 48 days, Kyrenia surrendered without a fight, as did the rest of the island, but Famagusta resisted to a degree that has become famous. The Turks, with an immense force of 100,000, approached along tunnels and trenches so deep that a man on horseback could not be seen, and so extensive that their entire army could disappear inside them. Using mines and artillery, the Turks commenced their firing, lobbing more than 150,000 cannon balls into the city. Inside, a force of a little over 5,000 men, Venetians, Cypriots and Albanian mercenaries, waited in terror behind the walls. Using clever tactics, making lots of brief sorties, the Venetian commander managed to trick the Ottomans into thinking that his troops were far more numerous, and the siege lasted an incredible ten months before the city fell, with the besieged, weak with plague and famine, reduced to eating cats and dogs. The Turks lost over 50,000 of their men in these ten months, and their rage on final victory was expressed in the most garish form. Surging through the gates, they overran

**Famous resistance**

**Ten-month siege** the entire place, randomly killing men, women and children, desecrating churches and plundering houses. The Venetian commander Bragadino, was flayed alive in public, having first had his nose and ears cut off, then his body was stuffed with straw to be sent to Constantinople dangling from the prow of a ship. The Turk, when roused, invariably earns his epithet 'terrible'. In Gazimağosa, the name the Turks use for Famagusta, the epithet 'Gazi' means Victorious Warrior, a title it earned when, in 1974, it held out against the Greek army.

\* **The Djambulat Tower**

Emerging from the outer wall circuit beside the

*Land Gate, old Famagusta*

Djambulat Tower, you can now turn left to enter the walls. The tower is named after one of the Turkish commanders of the siege. Here, the Venetians had erected a huge revolving wheel spiked with knives, on to which Turks were tossed as they scaled the walls, until the gully below was choked with dismembered bodies. Djambulat rushed at the wheel, and deliberately impaled himself and his horse on the huge grinding knife, thereby putting it out of action. His fellow soldiers were thus able to breach the defences.

**Gory heroism**

Today the tower holds his tomb and has been converted to a **small museum**, open 8.30am-1pm, 2.30-5pm, closed weekends. As a place of pilgrimage for Turks, this tower ranks second in Cyprus only to the shrine of Hala Sultan Tekke on the lake at Larnaca. The vaulted interior, with its huge long hall leading to the tower at the end, is in some ways more interesting than the exhibits. These include displays of guns, 17th century Turkish tiles and bowls, and some lovely 15th century Venetian plates. The attendant will give you the keys which enable you to climb the steps and get on to the roof, though there is no access to the ramparts.

**Place of pilgrimage**

**\*\***

## Othello's Tower

From the Djambulat you now continue along the dockside, passing the **Sea Gate** on the way to Othello's Tower. The Sea Gate was, along with the Land Gate, one of the two original gates of the walled city, and was built by the Venetians in 1496. The side that faces the harbour has a magnificent archway surmounted by a **Venetian lion** in a white marble gabled plaque. Since the gate is now closed, this is only visible from within the harbour itself. Beside the gate on the inside, towards the **Desdemona Gardens**, squats a handsome but eroded lion, carved out of a large stone block. Nearly opposite, the Petek Pastahanesi has a pretty upstairs area for **cakes and ice-cream**.

**White lion**

The emotively named 'Othello's Tower' is not just a tower. It would be more aptly called Othello's Castle, for it was built as a fort within a fort, a citadel

**A fort within a fort** to defend the entrance to the harbour. Its sea side now looks directly on to the quayside of the modern port, out of bounds to all but port traffic. In the pre-1974 days, when cruise ships and passenger ferries called at Famagusta, this citadel is the first thing that would have confronted visitors as the ship docked. Today, the ferries only come from Syria and Turkey.

The entrance to the tower today is from just inside the walls, through the gateway crowned by the white marble Venetian lion. The moat was drained of water on British instructions in 1900, because of the risk of malaria. Beside the gate is a **simple restaurant**, attractively set in green gardens with a playground. Opposite is the heavily ruined shell of **St George of the Latins**, a fortified 13th century church, the earliest church in the town. A little to the north, just inside the walls, is a football field marked on old maps of the 1960s as the Turkish polo field, 'Djirit'.

The tower has an entry fee and it takes a good half hour to have a proper look round inside, longer, if **Turkish cannon** you enjoy the fun of re-enacting Shakespeare. Scattered about in the open courtyard are **old cannon**. One, in Spanish bronze, is still rust free and in good condition. The others are mainly Turkish, recognizable by the heavy iron rings round the barrel. In several places, the iron cannon balls can be seen in piles, along with some stone balls that were tossed by the giant catapults.

Flanking the fine courtyard are the rooms of the citadel, regal in their proportions, especially the **Great Hall** or refectory, used in 1915 by Syrian refugees fleeing from the Turks.

Although Shakespeare had never visited Cyprus, probably indeed never left England's shores, he had evidently read of Sir Cristoforo Moro, who was **The Moor of Venice** sent by Venice to be governor of their colony of Cyprus in the early 1500s, and whose wife, to whom he was newly wed, died on her way from Cyprus. Othello the Moor of Venice was likewise sent by his masters...

*Duke.* 'The Turk with a most mighty preparation

makes for Cyprus. — Othello, the fortitude of the
place is best known to you; ... you must, therefore, be
content to slubber the gloss of your new fortunes with
this more stubborn and boisterous expedition.'

From Act II onwards, the setting is 'a seaport in
Cyprus'. Scene 3 of Act II takes place in 'a hall in the
castle', which must be the Great Hall or Refectory,
where much revelry and drinking was ordered by
Othello's herald.

** **Inside the walls**

Old Famagusta has a surprisingly quiet and unhurried
feel, though this is gradually changing as more shops
and cafés spring up to meet increasing tourist
demands. The flat dusty streets, the neglect, and the
randomly sprouting palm trees give the place a more
Middle Eastern feel than any other Cypriot town. Its
population has grown to something between 3,000 and
5,000, all of whom have been Turkish Cypriots ever
since the 16th century siege of Famagusta, when a
**Dusty** number of Turks stayed behind to colonise the island.
**Middle** The bombardments of the siege, however, along with
**Eastern** the destruction wrought when the place was finally
**town** overrun, were permanent scars, and in the 18th
century, travellers described it as miserable and
deserted, 'a confused mass of ruins and filth', with
scarcely 300 inhabitants. The Ottomans also used
Famagusta as a quarry: its ruined churches were
**Exports to** exported as stone blocks to Egypt, prompting the retort
**Egypt** that Alexandria is virtually Famagusta rebuilt in Egypt.

The state of the town and its churches cannot be
wholly laid at the door of the Turks however. In the
15th century, Venetian troops were quartered in
disused churches and private houses and, later on,
earthquakes also played their role. Today, an air of
dereliction continues to pervade the place, as the
husks of churches still tower above the modest low-
rise houses, and bombed-out open areas have never
filled up again.

Famagusta's name, from the Greek Ammochostos,
means Buried in the Sand, and its history was, up

**Buried in the sand**

until medieval times, as undistinguished as that implies. But when Acre, the last Crusader toehold in the Holy Land, fell to Saladin in 1291, Famagusta received an influx of new blood and burgeoned into sudden life. As the largest natural harbour on the island and also the closest to the Holy Land, it was the natural choice — Cyprus is the only land mass visible from the hills of Palestine. Protected from storms by the natural calm of the bay, Famagusta became virtually the only safe deep harbour left to

**Merchants**

Christendom in all the Levant. Suddenly the European kings and merchants were all concentrated here, and Famagusta quickly grew rich from its new role as middleman between east and west, import/export centre of the Mediterranean, trading in perfumes, spices and ivory from the east and selling the island's produce of sugar cane, wine and silk. On the crest of

**... and prostitutes**

the wave of wealth came the inevitable wave of immorality, and the city's prostitutes were said to be as wealthy — and as numerous — as the merchants. Hence the oft-repeated saying that Famagusta had 365 churches, each one paid for by a man or woman intent on buying their place in heaven. Famagusta's total of some 20 churches is indeed high, and many are explained by the plethora of sects that coexisted in the city. Here we have Latin and Greek, Maronite, Armenian, Coptic, Georgian, Carmelite, Nestorian,

**Plethora of sects**

Jacobite, Abyssinian and Jew. Of the 17 churches still standing today, only three are in use: the Nestorian church, now well-restored, has undergone a recent reincarnation as the Cultural Centre of the Eastern Mediterranean University of Famagusta; the church of St Peter and St Paul, now ingeniously converted to the municipal library; and the cathedral church of St Nicholas in service since the 16th century as Famagusta's main mosque, and now called Lala Mustapha Pasha, after the Ottoman Commander-in-Chief during the siege.

**\*\***

## The churches

To visit all the churches described in the following itinerary will take you two and a half to three hours on foot, but if you only have an hour, then just visit the central cluster round the main square, the Church of St Peter and St Paul, and the huge haunting shell of St George of the Greeks, once the Greek Orthodox Cathedral.

## ** Lala Mustapha Pasha mosque/St Nicholas Cathedral

Set in the main square in the heart of old Famagusta, the twin towers of the cathedral are visible from most parts of the old city. Making them even more distinctive is the misshapen minaret that tops one of them. There is usually somewhere to park in or around the main square, near the battery of taxi ranks, and this is the best place to begin your walking tour within the walls. An extensive restoration project began in 1993.

The imposing western façade of the cathedral has been likened to Rheims Cathedral in France, and it dominates the main square. Its towers were badly hit **Gothic** in the Turkish bombardment of the 16th century, and **grace** further damaged by earthquakes. Nevertheless, the cathedral is an undeniably beautiful building, its Gothic grace and elegance far exceeding that of its sister cathedral in Nicosia. It was built 100 years later than St Sophia, in the early 14th century, and its more **Delicate** delicate tracery work and ornate design reflect the **desgn** more luxurious lifestyle and tastes of the luxury-loving merchants of the port. The architects were themselves brought from France, and the cathedral may well have taken 100 years to complete. A tradition tells that the architects were a master and his pupil, and the master, on seeing the pupil's genius in the work, was consumed with jealousy. He invented a technical error he claimed to have noticed in the top of the towers, and having led the pupil up there to point out the error in detail, pushed him headlong over the edge — the first of much blood spilt at St Nicholas. The cathedral is built from the same familiar soft brown limestone that is used in the ramparts and walls. All **Old stone** the Crusader and Venetian buildings are from this stone and you need only walk round the town looking

*Lala Pasha mosque/St Nicholas, old Famagusta*

out for this colour to identify immediately all the older buildings.

The atmosphere of the square is much marred by an ugly hotchpotch of newer buildings and a plethora of telegraph poles and wires, inescapable from whichever direction you try to take a photo. To the left of the façade the small domed building that is now the Faisal Islamic Bank was once an **Ottoman madrasa**, built around 1700.

Foreign visitors to St Nicholas today must buy a ticket, the only one of the churches where this is the case. Inside, the whitewashed walls almost serve to **Church interior** emphasise the superb proportions and height of the nave. The stained glass was all blown out in the bombardment and blasting of the siege, save for the high rose window in the front façade. Today, the remaining colour is supplied by the mosque accessories, painted the usual reds and greens — the raised platform for the Koran recitation classes, the wooden pulpit or minbar, and the mihrab niche, indicating the direction of Mecca and around which all the decorative effort is concentrated, as in all mosques.

Your imagination has to work hard to recreate the splendid coronation ceremonies that took place here under the Lusignans. The custom had developed that each ruler was first crowned King of Cyprus in St Sophia in Nicosia, and then, after an elaborate and exhausting procession on horseback, was crowned King of Jerusalem here in St Nicholas, Famagusta being symbolically that bit closer to the Holy Land.

The huge old tree that looms to your right as you come out of the cathedral/mosque main door, is **Robust fig tree** thought to have been planted at the same time as the cathedral was built, i.e. around 1250. It is a type of tropical fig, originally from East Africa, and it keeps its foliage all year round except in February. The old **Venetian loggia** (open-sided arcade) facing the tree now serves as the mosque ablutions area. Beneath one of its two circular windows is a section of frieze with animals and garlands, taken from the cornice of a Roman temple, probably in Salamis.

**Rear view**

Behind the cathedral/mosque is a little **garden café** housed in a converted chapel, with tables and chairs scattered outside round a rudimentary fountain. Here you can sit and have a simple lunch of kebab and chips whilst overlooking the apse and buttresses of the cathedral. Youths are often clustered here playing backgammon, drinking coffee or coke. No beer or alcohol of any sort is on the menu, because the owner says that the government, with a baffling logic, will not permit the sale of alcohol on premises that were once a church.

## The Venetian Palace

**Casualty of the siege**

Opposite the cathedral, on the far side of the square, is the triple-arched façade of the 15th century Venetian Palace, supported by four granite columns which the Venetians brought from Salamis. This fragmentary relic is all that now remains of the once magnificent palace where the Venetian governor Bragadino lived. Its courtyard behind the arches was the stage for the excruciating death of the unfortunate Bragadino, (described earlier) a scene difficult to reconjure here in this peaceful and deserted spot. The building was badly damaged in the Turkish bombardment, and when the Turks took over the city, they did little to repair it. The section that still stood, on the west side, was turned into a police barracks, and it still serves this function today.

Beside the Venetian façade, just to the right, also facing into the main square, notice the little **Ottoman fountain** for distribution of drinking water. The basin is an adaptation of a Roman sarcophagus taken from Salamis.

**A poet's protest**

Unless you have a special interest in Turkish poetry, you can save yourself the visit to **Namık Kemal's prison** in the courtyard of the Venetian Palace. This writer and poet was locked up here for over three years for criticising the Sultan in Istanbul. Inside, there is nothing but four bare walls and an earth floor, while in the upstairs room are simply photos of Namık Kemal (1840-1888) and his contemporaries. His writings were political and patriotic, and he wrote articles, novels, plays and essays as well as poetry, reviling the stifling lifestyle under the last sultans, loathing the legacy of 600 years of stagnant cultural values.

Namık Kemal's bronze bust stands by the cathedral/mosque, facing the square.

## ** Church of St Peter and St Paul

Following the road away from the main square, leaving the Venetian Palace on your right, you soon reach the large tall church of St Peter and St Paul, unmistakable with its heavy flying buttresses, an essential prop for the high walls. It was built around 1360 and is still in a reasonable state of preservation because the Turks always found a use for it. It was at one time a mosque as evidenced by the ruined **Peaceful** minaret, missing its cone, built on to the southwest **library** corner. Under the British it was a grain and potato store. In 1964 it was restored and used as the town hall for a while, and it then served as Famagusta's **municipal library**, with a wonderfully pious atmosphere. Schoolchildren used to come here to do their homework in the peace and quiet that is difficult to find at home. The collections of books are an extraordinary hotchpotch. Standard works such as Shakespeare and Byron were ranged in cases alongside other lesser *ouevres* such as *Yoga for the West* and *The Love Letters of a Chinese Lady*. There was also a large collection of books in Greek, taken, one suspects, from houses after 1974. The church has now reverted to a mosque again.

## * The Nestorian Church

Walking on further, leaving the mosque on your left, you can now follow the road as it swings round gradually to the north (right) towards the cluster of five churches that lie near the western edge of the walls, and continue in a huge lap round the town before returning to the main square.

The first church you notice, down a side street opposite the Moratto Bastion, is the small pretty Nestorian church, neat and well-looked after in its

**Cultural** new role as the **Cultural Centre** of Famagusta's
**centre** Eastern Mediterranean University, the major
university of North Cyprus. Earlier, it was used as a
camel stable, though as recently as 1963, it still
served as a church. Its style is different to the other
churches, with its unusual but attractive **bell tower**
and small **rose window**. It was built for the Syrian
community of Famagusta by a wealthy businessman,
as many Nestorians were rich financiers. Inside, it
was decorated with frescoes by Italian and Syrian
painters of the 14th and 15th centuries, and it was
called St George the Foreigner to distinguish it from
St George of the Greeks and St George of the Latins.

## Out of bounds churches

Walking now beside the western rampart, the other
churches you pass are all within the fences of the
military zone that occupies the area round the
Martinengo Bastion. You can peer at them through the
fence, but unfortunately their murals and frescoes are
not visible from that distance.

**Ayia Anna** **Ayia Anna**, known locally as the church of the
Maronites, is the first of these churches, with a sturdy
belfry and a few frescoes inside. It is tiny but
beautifully proportioned. Next, on the corner, is the
**Tanner's Mosque**, originally a 16th century church.

On the other side of the road, within the camp
proper, is the tall Carmelite church of **St Mary**,
originally part of a monastery, now disappeared, for
the mendicant friars. It was richly adorned with
frescoes by Italian artists of the 14th and 15th
centuries, and some traces are said to remain. Behind
it stands the tiny 14th century **Armenian church**, said
to have frescoes and Armenian inscriptions still
visible.

**Church** Many of these churches suffered bad damage in the
**refuge** 1960s and 1970s, when Turkish Cypriots came here
as refugees having been turfed out of their villages by
the Greeks. Shortage of accommodation meant that
some had to camp inside the churches along with their
possessions and animals. Cooking fires caused
blackening and damage to frescoes, while children

larked about trying to prise off pieces of decoration with pen knives or to dislodge higher mosaics with catapults.

Some 300m beyond the Tanner's Mosque you now fork back south towards the main square to complete your circuit. On your right you can glance at the ruined **Kertikli Hammam**, a Turkish bath piled high with rubbish but with its six domes still intact.

**Biddulph's Gate**

Further on you pass on your right, just after a street junction, the structure known as **Biddulph's Gate**, an archway built from the old brown stone with three steps leading up into what was once the house of a wealthy merchant, but is now a small piece of open scruffy wasteland. Sir Robert Biddulph was the British High Commissioner in Cyprus in 1879 who stopped the gate being destroyed.

**Queen's House**

Beyond the next junction on the right, is one of the very few relics of a private as opposed to a public building, the shell of a **Venetian house**. The Venetians were only in Famagusta for 82 years and the bulk of their building effort went into the fortifications. The house's exterior is elegant and pleasing like all Venetian architecture in the style of Italian Renaissance. By peering through the keyhole you can see into the courtyard wilderness inside. Both doors are locked and the roof has collapsed. It used to be called the Queen's House.

Up a side street to the right, just before the Venetian house, you will come to the twin **churches of the Templars and the Hospitallers**, both branches of the Latin church formed at the time of the Crusades in 1350, yet often at loggerheads despite their apparent embrace. The left one has recently been converted to a private art gallery.

**A bath as a bar**

Just before the main square you pass the newly renovated **Djafer Pasha Hammam**, a Turkish bath built in 1601, now transformed into a trendy bar restaurant with tables and benches outside, overlooking the cathedral and the Venetian Palace. The thick glass pieces set into the roof allowed the sun in by day, and the starlight by night.

From the main square you can now head off south

to see the remaining four churches in a small loop. This route can also be driven, by taking the only permitted exit from the main square to the south, a narrow road which winds round to the right and takes you through a picturesque **Ottoman archway** like a gatehouse with rooms above.

**

## St George of the Greeks

The most impressive of these four southern churches by far is the huge shell of St George of the Greeks, standing alone in an area of wasteland. Its roof was blown off in the Turkish bombardment in 1571, and the most damaged part is visibly the side that faces the Djambulat Tower, the direction from which the Turkish artillery was firing. The pockmarking in the walls tallies with the size of the cannon balls. Many of these can still be seen lying about in the waste ground in and around the churches of this area. Some can be seen put to such ingenious uses as marking the edges of flower beds in houseproud gardens.

**Pock-marked shell**

You can enter the church from the western side, through a hole in the railings. It was built as the rival cathedral for Famagusta's Orthodox community. Its three apses once held frescoes showing the life of Christ, and some fragments survive in the eastern apse. In what remains of the roof, you can see the bottoms of pottery jars embedded. Their function is mysterious, but one ingenious suggestion is that they may have been to improve the acoustics.

Some 200m further to the south, also standing in open waste ground, are the two small 15th century churches of **Ayios Nicholas**, still with its roof but no frescoes inside, and further away, tucked behind it, the little dome of **Ayios Zoni**, a church in typical rustic Cypriot style. It is now kept locked to protect the fragmentary frescoes of the Archangel Michael, and you can just glimpse them if you peer in through cracks in the door.

**15th century churches**

The final church, further to the north, is the barrel-vaulted **Church of the Holy Cross** or Stavros, long used as a store, and later as a mosque.

** **TOWARDS VAROSHA**

Opposite the Land Gate outside the walls is a large modern roundabout, and it is from here that the wide road, previously known as **Independence Avenue**, leads off towards Varosha. In the centre of the roundabout stands a rather gory colossal bronze memorial, depicting the suffering of the Turks. Some 300m down this wide avenue on the left hand side, your eye may be caught by the little **steam locomotive** that stands just behind a wire fence in the garden of the **Varosha Police Station**. A plaque announces it was the first locomotive to be imported into Cyprus, in 1904. The little railway line on which it ran was the only one in Cyprus, built by the British, running from Famagusta via Nicosia to Morphou. There were passenger services, but very few Cypriots took advantage of them, being either too poor to afford a ticket, or content to travel more slowly by donkey or cart. The railway's primary function was to transport the copper and chrome from the Skouriotissa mines to the port at Famagusta, from where they were then exported. The coal on which they ran was brought all the way from England by boat. By 1945 the railway began to fall into disrepair, and diesel trucks were found to be more economical for transporting the copper ore. The last train ran in 1951.

**Only railway in Cyprus**

Following the road further south you soon come to the edge of Varosha, lying about 1km south of old Famagusta. Once the affluent Greek suburb, (*varoş* is Turkish for suburb), Varosha, the Monte Carlo of the Middle East, grew in the 1960s to be far larger than the old walled town. While the Turkish walled town decayed, this fashionable resort of Greek Cypriots and expatriates mushroomed with hotels and holiday flats along the 6km (4 mile) beach of Glossa, said to be the best beach in the eastern Mediterranean. By the early 1970s it had a population of 35,000, overwhelmingly Greeks. In March the annual Famagusta Orange Festival used to take place here, in which visitors were showered with oranges, as many as they could eat. Varosha was famous for its orange groves and

**Suburb to nowhere**

**Best beach**

**Famous fertility** fertile gardens, and the district had so many windmills it was sometimes called the Town of the Windmills.

Now fenced off and forlorn, it was evacuated in 1974 when the Turks captured it for use as a bargaining card in any future negotiations. There was no military necessity for its capture since no Turkish Cypriots lived there. On paper it is now in the hands of the UN, but in practice the Turkish Army uses one hotel as a barracks, another two as student hostels, and a further one as an officers' club. Furniture looting still goes on, despite the fence, and as you peer inside you can spot many houses where boarded up doors have been forced, window frames ripped out, and weeds are growing up through the floor. It is difficult to see how this or any other property formerly Greek could be returned. Here in Varosha, most of the houses would need total renovation and in some cases even demolition before starting again.

**Property nightmare** Where Greek houses have been used and inhabited in other parts of the north, many have been sold on to foreigners who have since spent much money on restoration. After 1974 the Turkish Cypriots were given Greek houses under a government scheme in compensation for property and land they lost in the south. They were issued with a paper which gave them title to it and they were then at liberty to sell it. In some cases there have been several sales of the same house since 1974 and to unravel all these transactions now would be a mighty task.

**Perimeter fence** You can drive south all the way along the edge of the fenced-off area, until you see the check-point barrier blocking your path: the Attila Line is just a kilometre or two beyond. You can return a slightly different way by forking off towards the sea whenever you can, hugging the Varosha fence throughout. In an unlikely clearing, strangely isolated from any other inhabited buildings, you will come upon **La Cheminée**, a chic French restaurant serving good food, evenings only.

Emerging near a sea lagoon, you will see another cluster of simpler restaurants facing out on to the modest yacht marina. On the headland beyond it is the luxury **Palm Beach Hotel**. Originally Greek-run and called the Constantia, the Palm Beach has been newly renovated and is the only high standard hotel that remains accessible in this part of Varosha. The other famous hotels, like the Grecian, the Florida and the King George, are all within the fence. The Greek Cypriots, ever mindful of a commercial opportunity, run cruises from Ayia Napa for tourists to stand off and peer at the ghost city. They also organise minibus or taxi trips to a viewing platform at the village of Dherinia, from where Varosha can be discerned through telescopes and binoculars.

*** **SALAMIS**

## Highlights

Ancient Salamis, the first city of Cyprus in classical Greek times, boasts some of the most **impressive classical monuments** to be found on the island. The pleasantly overgrown ruins lie among fragrant eucalyptus and acacia trees, alongside one of the island's finest beaches, with excellent and safe swimming. Situated some 9km (6 miles) north of Famagusta, it makes an easy visit and is readily accessible.

**Excellent beach**

The area covered by the site is huge, so huge that although archaeologists first began work here in 1890 and have continued intermittently throughout this century, the site is still only partially excavated. Networks of roads run across it, all unsignposted, and it is easy to lose your way, and difficult to get an overview as the site is so flat. A few minutes studying the map will help. A car is advisable, otherwise the full tour involves some 6 or 7km (4 miles) walking. In summer a visit can be blisteringly hot and the flat landscape offers precious little shade. Go well equipped with liquid refreshments or else you may find yourself hallucinating that the marble basins in the gymnasium are still sparkling with cool water.

**Partially excavated**

The site is open daily 8am-6pm. The main entrance for ticket sales closes at 3.30pm but the side entrance on the north stays open until after dusk to let you

**Timings**

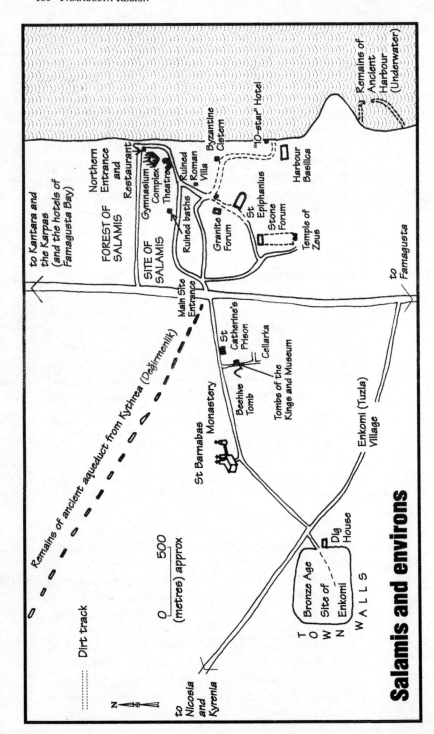

Salamis and environs

leave at your leisure. It takes about two to three hours to visit the major parts of the site, but you could easily spend a whole day here if you wanted to explore the site exhaustively. If you are coming from the Kyrenia area and only have a day to devote to Famagusta and its environs, you could spend the morning in old Famagusta, then drive on to Salamis for lunch at the pleasant seaside restaurant beside the northern site entrance. Those based in the Famagusta area will probably make separate visits to Salamis and the other sites close by. Recommended times for visits would be three to four hours for Salamis, two hours for the Tombs of the Kings and St Barnabas Monastery, and one hour for Enkomi.

## Touring Salamis

Heading north out of Famagusta towards Salamis, you pass, near the outskirts of town, a busy area with lots of cafés and pizza restaurants full of young people. Directly opposite is the reason — the **Eastern Mediterranean University**, North Cyprus' major university, offering degree courses in sciences, engineering, management and economics. The medium of instruction is English.

**Northern approach**

The road continues north until you reach the site after about 5km (three miles or so). There are two signposted entrances to Salamis. Ignoring the first, even though it seems the more major, continue to the second which takes you along the northern edge of the site and brings you out at the beach by the pleasant **restaurant** raised up overlooking the bay. Its spacious shady terrace makes a cool haven in summer, and in winter the indoor seating area is warm and cosy. Simple fare is on offer, like curry, kebabs and steak, and can be washed down with beer or wine. For the energetic, windsurfers are on hire on the beach opposite.

Buying your ticket at the barrier from one of the four brothers who have long been guardians at the site, you drive the car in and leave it at the first car parking area you come to, about 200m from the entrance. This is the closest to the baths/gymnasium

**The highpoint**

complex, and the theatre is just 100m further on. These two areas together form the most spectacular part of Salamis, the part you should explore most thoroughly. They have also received the bulk of the excavators' attention. Statues have been re-erected in the gymnasium and the theatre has been renovated. Though discovered in 1882 and dug erratically since then, the site was not excavated systematically until 1952. From then, work was in progress every season until 1974, when the University of Lyon excavators left.

There are still vast tracts of the city that await excavation, and in view of the current political situation the wait is likely to be a long one. Whenever it does happen, the task will be daunting, for Salamis was the victim of two severe earthquakes in the 4th century within ten years of each other. Tidal waves combed across the city bringing in sand and debris.

**Successive disasters**

Later that century, the Byzantine emperor Constantine II rebuilt it, but on a smaller scale, and renamed it Constantia in honour of himself. It suffered badly again in the Arab raids of the 7th century, and most of the population that survived the massacres moved to Famagusta, then called Arsinoe. Abandoned, its collapsed buildings were used as a quarry for medieval Famagusta, and the sand and vegetation reclaimed the city.

**\*\*\***

## The gymnasium and baths

The gymnasium is the pearl of Salamis and the glimpse of lifestyle afforded here helps convey more than any other monument yet exposed the magnificence and wealth the city must have enjoyed in Hellenistic and Roman times. As you first enter along the marble pavements, you feel the elegant colonnaded courtyard must have been the forum, the market place and heart of the city, rather than simply an outbuilding devoted to education and the culture of the body, the ancient Greek version of a school and health centre. It is now thought there were originally three gymnasia, two for boys and one for girls. The open forecourt (palaestra) was where the boy athletes would

**Lavish body culture**

exercise and train. Afterwards they would plunge in the cool water of the two pools, watched by the naked white marble statues of their gymnasiarchs or headmasters. These were wealthy citizens who were elected for a one year term to help with the school's finances, and also provided the expensive olive oil for body massage for those boys who had won free attendance by scholarship. Today these gymnasiarch statues have been replaced by women draped in robes, **Headless** headless to a woman, decapitated by early Christian **statues** zealots, the Muslim fundamentalists of their day, who took the statues to be relics of the pagan religion. Nudity offended them, and all bare statues were broken up or tossed into drains. Clothed statues were just tolerable if their faces were removed. Today the most striking statue is the handless and faceless black marble Persephone.

**Curious** The columns of the porticoes were re-erected in the **columns** 1950s by the excavators, and on close examination, the apparent harmony of the whole reveals its mixed origins, for it was destroyed and re-erected many times in its history. In the east portico, for example, the Corinthian capitals are too small for their columns, which are taller and larger than this on the other three sides, presumably brought from somewhere else in the city by the later Byzantine builders.

The Hellenistic and Roman latrines are situated in the southwest corner of the palaestra, and are the **Open plan** largest on the island. Arranged in a semi-circle, with **latrines** open plan seating for 44, they strike us today, with our prudishly solitary cubicles, as most improper. The puritanical Christians of the 4th century, too, considered them indecent, and had them walled up.

Beside the gymnasium are the colossal **Byzantine baths**, so deeply buried in sand they were only discovered in 1926, an impressive complex of tall chambers with marble and mosaic flooring and underfloor heating. In two of the vaulted arches traces of Roman mosaics can still be seen, mainly in reds and browns. In the largest mosaic, the central figure is thought to be Apollo with a lyre and quiver below.

*Salamis*

The walls throughout are of immense thickness, often 3m or more. Columns and capitals lie scattered about, but much of the more elaborate marble carving was taken away and is now on display in the Cyprus Museum of Greek Nicosia. Some of the finds used also to be on display at the Museum of Famagusta within the suburb of Varosha. Now they are doubtless heavily cobwebbed. The intricate water system, here and in the gymnasium, is a perpetual source of amazement. A 56km (35 mile) long aqueduct brought water from the abundant spring at Kythrea (now Değirmenlik) to a large tank which can still be seen in the undergrowth (see map). Scholars have estimated that this water system could supply the needs of 120,000 people.

**Amazing aqueduct**

**\*\***

## The theatre

**The largest on the island**

The theatre was not discovered until 1959 and archaeologists have now rebuilt it to under half its original height, 18 of the 50 rows of seats. Of these, only the first eight rows are original, and the division is clear where their white limestone casing gives way to the brown limestone used in the reconstruction. Badly damaged in the earthquakes of the 4th century, many of its original stones and decorative blocks were carted off for reuse in other buildings. The marble tiles of its orchestra for example were taken off to renovate the nearby baths after an earthquake. The channel in the middle of the orchestra was the drainage for blood from animals sacrificed to Dionysus before each performance. With an original seating capacity of between 15,000 and 20,000 it is far and away the largest theatre in Cyprus, reflecting the fact that Salamis was the foremost city on the island for much of its history. The modern wooden cabins beside the orchestra are kitted out with portaloos when the theatre is used occasionally for school plays or concerts.

Most of the extant ruins today date from the Roman and Byzantine times, but Salamis was in fact founded in the 12th century BC by a hero of the Trojan War. Brother to Ajax, his name was Teucer, and he named

**Trojan founder** the new Greek colony in Cyprus after the small island of Salamis (near Piraeus) which had been his homeland. All over the island, other heroes of the Trojan War also founded their own cities, such as Paphos, Soli, Lapithos, Kyrenia, Marion (Polis), and each was independent, ruled by its own king. At one time there were ten such tiny kingdoms on the island. Salamis was generally the most powerful, and by virtue of its excellent harbour, became the greatest commercial centre, trading with the Levant, Greece and Rome. It was the first city in Cyprus to mint its own coinage.

** ## The harbour basilica

After the gymnasium and theatre area, the next most impressive section of ruins at Salamis is to be found beside the old Roman harbour. To reach them, you head south from the theatre, forking left at the first junction of tarmac roads. Some 100m or so after this junction on the left of the road is an **underground Byzantine cistern** with paintings on the walls, but now kept locked. The key is held by the Famagusta **Byzantine cistern** Department of Antiquities, beside the Namık Kemal prison. The cistern consists of three interconnecting chambers, in one of which are faded water scenes of fish and sea plants with a bearded Christ above. Access involves descending a ladder with torches.

Beyond the cistern, as the road heads toward the sea, you will see rising up on your right, the columns of the recently excavated but already overgrown basilica identified as **Campana Petra**, standing just above the sandy beach. The large attractive building has been dated to the 4th century, and has elegant columns and many beautiful geometric floor designs. **Modern style mosaics** The bulk of the stone is white marble, and in summer the impression is of dazzling brightness as the sun glints off the sea and the gleaming stone. The most elaborate floor patterning of all is to be found in the lowest section of the basilica near the sea, where the diamond-shaped stones are set in very modern looking swirls of colour.

After exploring the basilica, you can go on to the

beach for a swim or to seek out the remains of the Roman harbour. In the clear shallow water are thousands of fragments of Roman sherds, and beyond, the harbour wall is still only at waist height. The main harbour of ancient Salamis in fact lies a little further south, and you can explore it by strolling along the beach and rounding the first headland.

**10 star hotel**

Just to the left where you first come on to the beach from the basilica, is the relic of the imaginative '10 star Hotel', run by Ali Sager for the last 15 years. Made from the shell of a military concrete bunker, Ali ingeniously endowed his hotel with all mod-cons devised from beach-combing: tables and chairs from slabs of spare stone, tied round with cardboard for warmth on bare skin; windmills made from bits of twig and rope and a King Edward cigar packet; a bicycle bell at the gate, and numerous other bits of bric-à-brac whose functions you could spend hours guessing at. A refugee from Larnaca, Ali worked in the harbours of Kyrenia and Famagusta before retiring to become harbour master of Salamis. During the day, he used to offer simple *mezze* to his tourist visitors and his pet lizards, and in the evening he went home to his wife who, like most wives in Cyprus, never visited her husband's workplace.

## The Stone Forum, St Epiphanius and the Granite Forum

Today there are still three more monuments in addition to those already described, which impress despite their heavily ruined and unexcavated state. For those with the time, it is pleasant to stroll around the ancient city to find them, enjoying the gentle breeze which blows in the fragrant eucalyptus trees. In spring and early summer, the walk across the gentle rise and fall of the land is especially lovely, alive with the yellow blossom of acacia mimosa.

Most memorable perhaps, is the **Stone Forum**, thought to be the largest forum or market place in the entire Roman Empire, measuring 230m by 55m. It is best viewed from the temple end (see map), after parking in the shade under the clump of trees where

**Gigantic market place**

the track finishes. It is so heavily overgrown that you must pick your way across to the temple podium, slightly raised, from where you can then look out over the forum. The column stumps lining the sides are still visible and a solitary capital remains on its full height column to help evoke the scale of the whole. The **little temple**, whose well-crafted marble steps are still visible, is known to have been dedicated to Zeus (Jupiter), who was also the protector of the island of Salamis, the city's namesake. At the far end of the forum is the deep, pillared reservoir that supplied the city, another good viewing point for the forum.

Returning to the track that winds northwards past the end of this reservoir, you will come on your right to an iron gate leading into a fenced-in area that contains the foundations of **St Epiphanius**, the largest basilica in Cyprus. It was built in 345, just after the earthquakes, by Epiphanius, the bishop of Constantia. Utterly devastated as it is, the church still conveys its vastness. Salamis has an important place in the early history of Christianity, and St Barnabas was himself born here. Barnabas accompanied Paul on his first missionary journey from Antioch:

**Barnabas, missionary and martyr**

> 'We preached Christ crucified, unto the Jews a stumbling block and unto the Greeks foolishness... For the Jews require a sign, and the Greeks seek after wisdom.' (Corinthians)

Later Barnabas split from Paul and came to Cyprus again with his nephew, the young John Mark. He became, according to church tradition, the first bishop of the Church of Cyprus, and was martyred by the Jews of his native Salamis in 75AD. On the site where he is buried, the St Barnabas monastery now stands, described a little later.

Close to the basilica, just a little further north on the opposite side of the road, look out for the huge tumbled granite columns of another **forum**. These hefty 50 ton 6m long columns are in the unmistakable pinkish colour of Aswan granite from Egypt. Nearby on the other side of the road, some maps mark a

**Elusive water clock** 'water clock'. Don't excite yourself however, for there is nothing to be seen beyond a cluster of stones covered in undergrowth. The original is thought to have been a still pool reflecting the stars, thus telling the time at night.

Even more difficult to spot in the undergrowth are the fragmentary blocks of a **Roman villa**. All around are more buildings, covered in sand and undergrowth, awaiting excavation. Sections of town wall belonging to the smaller Byzantine town of Constantia can be glimpsed here and there. Of the earlier Greek city wall, nothing remains except earth banks. Just opposite the main entrance to Salamis, you can still **Aqueduct** see in the scrubland a fragment of the **aqueduct** that brought water down from Kythrea. At the beginning of the century, parts of it were still in use.

## * THE TOMBS OF THE KINGS
## THE NECROPOLIS OF SALAMIS

### Highlights
This is an unusual collection of tombs, unique on the island, interesting for their strange Homeric associations. They are less than 1km from the main site of Salamis.

The gates to the tomb enclosures are usually open, but the adjacent little museum is only open from 8am-4pm weekdays. A visit of half an hour will suffice.

### Touring the Tombs of the Kings
Leaving Salamis by the inland site gateway, the road that continues inland after a short left/right dogleg takes you to the necropolis of Salamis after just 500m or so on your left, with the St Barnabas Monastery 1km further inland on the same road.

There are six major **royal tombs** and a visit to all would take at least an hour. If you are short of time you might confine yourself to two: St Catherine's Prison and Tomb No 47.

The tomb known as **St Catherine's Prison** is unmistakable, with its stone vaulted hump, and is also

**St Catherine's Prison**

the first tomb you reach from Salamis, just to the left of the road. You can park and enter it from the road, as it is slightly set apart from the main tomb cluster further on. Its unique appearance is because the Romans built a chapel above the original tomb, using these huge stone blocks, and dedicated it to St Catherine. Inside, pieces of church furniture like lecterns and tables still lie in alcoves. Another alcove, to judge from the smell, is used as a latrine.

**Too perfect to marry**

St Catherine, the early Christian martyr of Alexandria, was born in Salamis, daughter to one of the island's puppet kings under Roman administration. She refused to marry unless her parents found her a groom as fair and learned and wise and rich as herself. Her parents considered this impossible and sent her to a holy hermit, who told her the only man she could marry with these conditions was Jesus Christ. Her father was later exiled to Alexandria and the Christians on the island severely tortured. Catherine proclaimed herself of the faith and was thrown in prison, and later sent to Alexandria herself, to be martyred between two columns on a wheel. When the site was excavated in 1965, it was shown to be of the same type as the others in the necropolis, dated to the 7th century BC. Like them, it has the skeletons of a pair of royal horses yoked together in the entrance passage, sent to the afterlife with their master.

**Museum**

Some 100m further inland a yellow sign announces the **Tombs of the Kings**, and you turn left on to the small tarmac road that leads to the little **museum** and ticket office. Both these are closed at weekends, but you can usually still gain access to the tombs themselves, as their gates are not generally locked. If the museum is shut, you can peer in through the windows to see the reconstructions of the bronze horse chariots and drawings showing the course of excavations, and how the tombs were found. The discovery of these tombs and their accompanying chariots has yielded the evidence for confirming Salamis' origins as a Trojan foundation, and Homer's Iliad describes precisely such funeral pyres as were found here, piled high with jars of honey and oil, and then the four horses on top.

The two tombs on the same side of the road as the museum, 47 and 79, are the most interesting. On their wide sloping entrance passages are the skeletons of the horses which had pulled the king's hearse to the grave. The skeletons are now preserved under glass cases like vegetables. The king's body was cremated and the horses were then sacrificed, still yoked together. Their death agony is evident in their contorted positions, their necks broken and twisted in panic.

**Yoked horses**

On the opposite side of the road, the huge anthill mound with a modern gabled roof of asbestos is prominent. This was imaginatively christened **Tomb No 3** by the archaeologists working the site in the 1960s. Inside, you simply clamber down to the empty grave chamber. The remaining tombs lie behind the beehive No 3, in fenced-in areas. They are in a sorry state, overgrown and vandalised, the glass skeleton cases smashed, scarcely warranting the extra walk for the non-specialist.

## * The Çellarka

More interesting in many ways to those who have the time, is the short detour to visit the additional group of tombs known as the Çellarka. This is an area some 15m by 100m dug out in a maze of interlinking underground tombs, at least 50 in all. Some are approached by **rock cut steps** down to the grave chamber, and one of the tomb doorways has simple decoration with what looks like a fish carved into the rock.

**Maze of tombs**

To reach the Çellarka you simply continue along the tarmac road beyond the museum for 100m or so, then fork left up an overgrown tarmac road lined with oleander bushes. You arrive at an area fenced-in and with the door locked, but under a large eucalyptus tree to the left, the fence is down and you can enter. Don't go round these tombs after a beer too many at lunchtime, lest you slip and entomb yourself.

**Mind your step**

\*  # ENKOMI
## BRONZE AGE CAPITAL OF CYPRUS

### Highlights

Enkomi, the first ancient capital of the island, dated to 2000BC, is a much underrated site. Even though at first glance it looks uninspiring, the longer you stay down inside the site, the more you notice the details which gradually bring it alive. Allow anything from 30 minutes to an hour.

### Touring Enkomi

To reach the site you drive inland (west) from the Tombs of the Kings towards the St Barnabas Monastery whose church tower and domes are visible about 1km away in the distance. Just at the brow of a small hill past the monastery you will see a cluster of derelict buildings on the left among some trees, and this is the entrance to the site. These buildings were the **French excavators' headquarters** for the digs that went on here under Professor Schaeffer (excavator of Ugarit/Ras Shamra in Syria) from the 1930s until the 1960s. The site was in fact first excavated in 1896 by the British, who found quantities of treasure and Mycenean pottery, now in the British Museum.

**Early digs**

The site has, since the late 1960s, unfortunately fallen into neglect, and the ticket office that was is now closed up. There are no toilets or refreshments available, but there is still a bench near the parking area above the site from which the faint-hearted can sit and look.

The whole site is remarkably large, about 1km square, as befits the ancient capital of Cyprus or 'Alassia' as it was called then. Its main trade was in copper ingots, notably with the pharaohs of Egypt and the Hittites of Asia Minor, and Professor Schaeffer also found much evidence of Enkomi's role as a staging post between the Mycenean towns of the Aegean and the towns of the Syrian coast. The merchants grew wealthy on this trade, and the prosperity is visible in the strikingly grand and well-

**Wealthy trading centre**

built houses for this early period of history.

Follow the old path down into the site and walk first along the main street, looking out for the **houses** built of large and well-crafted blocks. The whole town is littered with fragments of sherds and greeny black **Abundant** pieces of stone lying about on the tops of the walls for **wells** the picking. Abandoned by human visitors, the site is alive with lizards and birdlife. All around, you will come across wells, grinding stones and cisterns. One well, some 7m deep, still has water, and you can see evidence of a remarkably sophisticated **water-system**. Especially impressive are the huge door lintel blocks, and the vast door openings, sometimes 3m wide, notably into the so-called **House of the Pillar**, to the right of the main street.

Also to the right of the path, look out for the large stone block in the shape of bull's horns, highly **Bull horns** reminiscent of the Minoan fertility symbol. The building in which it stands is known as the **Sanctuary of the Horned God**, and it was here that the little bronze horned statue of a god was found, often seen on pictures and now in the Cyprus Museum.

**House of** In another large house known as the **House of the** **Bronzes** **Bronzes** to the left of the main street, many finely wrought bronze objects were unearthed by the French in the 1930s, and now also in the Cyprus Museum. At the extremities of the site, particularly in the north and south, large sections of the town wall can still be seen, with the foundations of fortified city gate towers.

## *  ST BARNABAS MONASTERY

### Highlights

St Barnabas (Ayios Varnavas) Monastery, along with Ayias Mamas in Güzelyurt and Apostolos Andreas on the Karpas tip, is a complete monastery preserved as it was pre-1974 and open for viewing as an icon museum. Its atmosphere is relaxed and pleasant, and it lies less than 2km from Salamis.

A visit takes at least 40 minutes. There are toilets here and a recently opened café in the gardens. Entry **Timings** tickets are sold by one of the Salamis guardian brothers, and the likeness is evident. It is open daily, generally open from 8am-5pm or later in the summer.

## Touring St Barnabas monastery

Set on the road between Enkomi and the Tombs of the Kings, a signpost announces the monastery and you drive up to the door opposite the attractively carved **water fountain**.

**Team of brothers**

The monastery was functioning until 1976, having been lived in since 1917 by three monks, all brothers, said to be indistinguishable from one another. The youngest, a mere 79, was a painter, producing quantities of tasteless icons which were sold to visitors to drum up money for the repairs needed in the monastery. The other brothers, despite their age, then effected these repairs, adding the **new bell tower** and finishing the rooms and cells around the courtyard. As you enter the monastery through its blue gates, you will notice a photo of the three brothers. One died and the others returned to Stavrovouni in Greek Cyprus.

**Pretty cloisters**

The attractive garden and **cloister courtyard** contains quantities of carved blocks and capitals from Salamis, and an impressive black basalt grinding mill from Enkomi. Many of the rooms around the courtyard are bursting with pottery from the Enkomi site, and others contain icons collected from the churches of surrounding villages. Some of these icons are now on display. The **courtyard garden** is still well-tended, with jasmine and hibiscus flame trees, huge pink flowering cacti and citrus trees, one of which is a hybrid producing oranges, lemons and mandarins from different parts of the same tree. Refreshments are on offer here.

**Modern frescoes**

The **monastery church** itself is preserved exactly as it was when the monks left. The pulpits, wooden lecterns and pews are still in place, and the icons and frescoes on the walls are still as they were. The newer, crasser ones are the work of the prolific brother. A series of four depict the story of how the Cypriot Archbishop went to Constantinople to request and be granted independence for the Church of Cyprus by the Emperor Zeno. This story is especially pertinent to the monastery, as it was thanks to Barnabas that this came about. Barnabas, born in Salamis, returned here later with Paul and died in his native town, martyred by the Jews. As the apostle who, with Paul, brought Christianity to Cyprus, Barnabas is revered as the real founder of the Cypriot Church, and when his bones were discovered here in 477, the Archbishop set off to Constantinople to ask that the Cypriot Church be granted its independence. The Byzantine Emperor agreed, persuaded by the gift of the original Gospel of St Matthew, in Barnabas' own handwriting, allegedly found clasped in the dead saint's arms. Zeno even donated the funds for this, the first monastery on Cyprus. Today, the self-governing Church of Cyprus ranks fifth in the world of Greek Orthodoxy — after the Patriarchates of Constantinople, Alexandria, Antioch and Jerusalem, but before the Patriarchates of Russia, Greece, Serbia, Rumania, etc.

**Ancient icon**   The monastery as it stands now dates largely to the 18th century, as the original 5th century building was destroyed in the Arab raids. Of the icons in the church, one, to the left of the iconostasis portraying two men, is said to be 1,000 years old. Carved capitals from Salamis peep out from the whitewashed walls, and the blackened pillar inside the painted apse is also from Salamis. Near the altar are **wax effigies** of an arm, a foot, and even a head, from families whose children have illnesses in these parts of the body, hung here for the saint to cure.

**Ingenious kennel**   Outside the monastery, round the side towards the bell tower are some older ruined outbuildings, now disused except by a dog which has ingeniously turned a carved **Roman sarcophagus** into a kennel for its puppies.

The tree-lined road straight ahead from the monastery door leads to Barnabas' tomb. The plain domed mausoleum was erected in the 1950's above an old rock tomb, and you can still clamber down the rock steps to see this empty tomb where the bones of Barnabas and his gospel of St Matthew were said to have been found.

# CHURCHES IN THE MESAORIA PLAIN

Scattered about in the countryside or in the villages of the Mesaoria Plain are a few other churches which enthusiasts may care to visit. They can be seen in a two hour circuit from a starting point of Boğaz or Salamis, and the drive also affords the chance to see the deeply rural communities of the plain whose lifestyle is so far removed from that of the towns and cities close by.

**Rural lifestyle**

Starting inland from Famagusta towards Iskele (Greek Trikomo, birthplace of George Grivas Dighenis 1878-1973, the EOKA leader), you come in the very heart of this pretty little rural town to the tiny but perfectly preserved **Dominican chapel of St James**, nearly bisected by crossroads, like a sort of traffic island. Its tiny floor area and relatively high dome give it a distinctly Armenian look. It is now kept locked to protect the 15th century interior and the porcelain plates set in its vaulted ceiling.

**Tiny gem**

Heading out west from Iskele on the Geçitkale/ Nicosia road, you will come to the 12th century domed church of **Panayia Theotokos**, now converted to an icon museum. Inside, it also has traces of 12th and 15th century wall paintings.

Sınırüstü (Greek Syngrasis) is the next village you come to, strikingly set under a small escarpment with the occasional palm tree peeping out of the fertile greenery. Here you turn left (south), and as you leave the village outskirts, you will notice on your left a domed church surrounded by a cluster of cypress trees, approached by a derelict tarmac lane. This is the 13th century **Ayios Prokopius**, and it is open and empty but for a few wooden pulpits and pews. The interior has two large frescoes of St George and the Dragon on a deep blue background, and opposite is an older fresco of a saint on a horse.

**Derelict frescoes**

Returning to the Sınırüstü junction you now continue west towards **Geçitkale**, a large town of the plain. Its recently opened airport tends only to be used when Ercan is closed for repairs. Just before the village of Akova (Greek Gypsos), you will pass a

**New airport**

desecrated Greek cemetery on the left of the road. Beside it is a new Turkish cemetery with the first graves dated 1987.

Turn left (south) at Akova and at the next village, Yıldırım (Greek Milea), turn left again to head back towards the coast. Leaving the outskirts of the village, the medieval church of **Ayios Yeoryios** is to be found to the right of the road.

Also on the right some 3km further on, set a good 500m off the road and not visible from it, is the 17th century **Panayia Avgasida** monastery, 1km northeast of Şehitler (Greek Sandlaris), with a double-aisled domed church.

**Numerous churches**

The striking thing with all these churches is how numerous they are: the tiniest village usually boasts a church and it is quite common for larger villages to have two or three. The reason for this lies in Cyprus' history, where the church long represented political power as much as religious devotion. During this century the church bells were used by Greek Cypriot EOKA zealots as summons or as danger signals. All the churches are now derelict, or if their location lends itself, they are turned into barns or stables.

**... and few mosques**

Mosques, on the other hand, are few and far between: recent surveys have confirmed that Turkish Cypriots are among the least zealous Muslims in the world.

Loggerhead sea turtle, now the subject of several conservationist projects

## Chapter Six

# The Karpas Peninsula

*** **Highlights**

The Karpas has been called the nature reserve of
Cyprus, with abundant wildlife and flowers, as yet
untouched by encroaching development. Remote and
isolated by virtue of its geographical position, it holds
itself aloof from the rest of the island, and almost
feels like a different country. The peninsula was
predominantly Greek pre-1974, and boasts some
exquisite early churches which should not be missed.
A few are still in use, as the Karpas retains a small
community of Greeks, some 600 strong, who chose to
stay behind after 1974, and they continue to live in
and around Dipkarpaz (Greek Rizokarpaso). The rural

**The end of
the earth**
landscapes are but sparsely populated, and as you
drive out towards the ever-narrowing tip, you feel you
are driving to the end of the earth.

The corollary of its isolation is that accommodation
and restaurants are few and far between in the Karpas,
so it is best to go well-equipped and self-sufficient, or
plan ahead to build your itinerary round the available
facilities. North of Boğaz, the only recommended

**Sparse
facilities**
accommodation is the Blue Sea Hotel some 10km (6
miles) beyond Dipkarpaz, and the Florya annexe
rooms midway between Yeni Erenköy and Dipkarpaz.
Both of these are also restaurants, and otherwise there
are just a few restaurants mainly along the road
between Yeni Erenköy and Dipkarpaz. Petrol stations
are also scarce and it is best to set off with a full tank
and fill up when you can.

It takes at least two days to explore the Karpas
properly, especially if you are coming from Kyrenia.

**Timings**  The drive from Kyrenia to Dipkarpaz takes about three hours, whereas from Salamis it takes less than two, and from Boğaz, one and a half. These timings are based on a gentle pace suited to the narrow winding roads. An early start is essential.

## Touring the Karpas Peninsula
### In general

Those who can only devote a day to the Karpas should head out beyond Dipkarpaz to Ayios Philon and Aphendrika, then drive on for lunch at the Blue Sea Hotel and take a quick look at the Apostolos Andreas monastery. On the way back, call off at Ayia Trias in the Greek village of Sipahi. Kanakaria church is kept locked, and the key has to be extracted from the village *muhtar* or headman, so that is best left for

**Itinerary planning**  an occasion with plenty of time. There are many other minor churches and sites, and the more leisured visitor can take his pick from the following itinerary.

### In detail

The Turks, ever since Sultan Selim first took a fancy to 'the rock called Cyprus', have regarded the island as an extension of Anatolia. The long tapering peninsula that reached up to the north east was described by Churchill as 'the dagger which points at the soft underbelly of Turkey'. If you choose to see in the landmass of Cyprus, the shape of an oblong frying pan, you could choose to see in the Karpas the shape of the panhandle. Viewed this way rather than as a dagger, the handle is conveniently turned towards Turkey, the master who can seize it and take control.

**Pottering along the Panhandle**  The peninsula falls into **three distinct sections**: first, from the fishing village of Boğaz to Ziyamet, the least interesting section, forming a kind of transitional zone from the mainland; next, from Ziyamet to Dipkarpaz, scenically much prettier with smaller roads and more contours, this section also has the much publicised Kanakaria church and the early Ayia Trias basilica with its mosaic floor; finally there is the section beyond Dipkarpaz, definitely the most rewarding stretch, with the northern fork to Ayios

Philon and Aphendrika, and the southern fork to the Apostolos Andreas monastery and Kastros at the very tip. In an ideal world, this section would warrant an entire day in itself, with time to enjoy one of the many deserted beaches, something that is best achieved by spending the night at the Blue Sea Hotel.

## TO ZIYAMET

The first section of the Karpas, before Ziyamet, has the largest number of sites to visit, albeit minor, and for those with the time and inclination to explore fully, there are three possible detours from the main road.

Starting at Boğaz, the first is at the turn-off right (south) towards the west at Kalecık. There is no signpost but the landmark is the group of oil storage tanks visible some kilometres away on the coast. Kalecık means 'little castle' (Greek Gastria) and by the sea near the tanker terminal are the heavily ruined **Crusader** 12th century twin templar castles of **Kastros** and **remains** **Strongylos**. A few foundations and cisterns are all that remain today. Nearby is the ruined chapel of **Ayios Ioannis**. In the village itself, the school is a former Byzantine church. Kalecık is the second port of North Cyprus after Famagusta and before Kyrenia, used for exporting quantities of cargo, especially the tobacco grown in the Karpas, and for importing oil. It has no passenger traffic.

At Tuzluca, the village on the crossroads to the north, the curious can seek out the large stone to be found in the old churchyard. The stone has a hole in the middle and local tradition held that every Easter **Test of** Monday, if the married men of the village clambered **fidelity** through the hole, they could check that their wives had remained faithful. Any that had been cuckolded got stuck because of their 'horns' and having extricated themselves, rushed off to beat their wicked spouses and begin divorce proceedings. Records show that the last such event occurred in 1935. With scarcely 600 inhabitants one would have thought the opportunities for infidelity were limited, and the chances of keeping it quiet even more limited.

At Çaylrova (Greek Ayios Theodhoros), the next village on the way to Ziyamet, an 8km long dirt track forks south to the headland of Zeytin Burnu, Olive Cape (Greek Cape Elea). Here, to the right of the track, close to the sea, are the ruins of ancient **Seaside ruins** **Phoenician Cnidus** set in a natural harbour. Today they are scarcely visible among the ploughed fields, but the town was inhabited from the 5th century BC until the 2nd century AD.

From Çaylrova you can take the fork to the north to the village of Zeybekköy, then to the right again to the hamlet of Sazlıköy (Greek Livadhia). At the foot of the hill behind this village, set alone in a bucolic setting you will see the pretty little church of **Panayia tis Kyras**, thought to be 7th century. It can be approached from a track to the left that starts directly opposite the mosque, but most of the last section has **Cure for pimples** to be done on foot, about five minutes across the fields. Empty and desecrated, it has a little arched side entrance with a charming sitting area. Inside there was a mosaic of the Virgin, now largely disappeared as a result of the local superstition that a cube of the mosaic would, if kept in a pocket, banish pimples and spots.

A fork south from Çaylrova leads to the village of Bafra, and beyond to a sandy bay where an uncompleted holiday village stands awaiting its fate. Further north at Kumyalı a fork off to the harbour **Pelican Club** leads to a sandy beach with the **Pelican Club** restaurant. In the village itself, raised up on a hillock, is a small 15th century church built above an ancient tomb, and all around are vestiges of a classical necropolis.

## BEYOND ZIYAMET

At Ziyamet (Greek Leonarisso) the character of the Karpas changes, becoming much more rural and hilly. Ziyamet, a small town inhabited largely by mainland Turks, is also a crossroads, where a fork right to Gelincik will take you to the monastery church of

Kanakaria. This fork continues all the way to Kaleburnu, but the track marked on most maps between Kuruova and Sipahi is terrible and any ideas you may have of a shortcut to Sipahi should be abandoned. Even if you had a jeep, the going is so slow that it is quicker to return to Ziyamet and double back on the tarmac.

**Kanakaria Church**

The large Byzantine monastery church of **Panayia Kanakaria** stands on the left of the road soon after entering the village of Boltaşlı (Greek Lythrangomi). A battered old red sign, scarcely legible, announces it in Greek and in English. The monastery outbuildings are gradually decaying and in the graveyard round the back, three desecrated graves of the last monks peep out above the weeds. In the semi-circular ceiling above the main entrance is a well-preserved **fresco** of the Virgin dated 1779. The original 11th to 12th century church was restored at that time, giving the church stone a newish look.

**Infamous mosaic theft**

The door is kept locked but you can go into the village to ask the muhtar or headman for the key if you are really keen. Inside, a fragment of a mosaic of the Virgin and Child in the central apse was all that survived of the earliest 5th or 6th century church, making this the **earliest Byzantine mosaic** on the island. This is the fragment that was stolen on the instructions of black market art dealers. Four sections, each measuring 61cm square, were chipped away. They depicted the Christ Child, an angel, and the saints James and Andrew. On the black market for antiquities they found their way to Indianapolis, to an art dealer who paid $1.1 million for them. She in turn tried to sell them to the J Paul Getty Museum in California for $20 million, but Getty's curator notified the Cypriot authorities. The autonomous Greek Orthodox Church of Cyprus and the Republic of Cyprus brought the court case against the art dealer to try to get them restored to the island, and this is the court case which hit the press in 1989.

By standing on piles of stones outside the apse windows, you can just about peer inside to glimpse the badly damaged interior. Traces of fresco can still be made out on the walls, but the pigeons have taken over wholesale.

The drive further along this little road towards Kaleburnu is interesting for its scenery, rather than the sites along it, which are essentially minor. The stretch between Derince and Avtepe is most unusual, with a dramatic drop down into a huge valley and bare rolling hills all around. A track leads along this river valley to the sea, some 4km away, where a ruined 14th century domed chapel, **Ayios Seryios**, can still be seen, to the right of the river mouth. Northeast of Avtepe there is also an unusual **cave tomb** of unknown date cut into a bare cliffside at a height of some 200m, and visible as you approach from afar. The climb up to it is very tricky and should only be attempted by those who relish heights and unsure footholds. Inside, are many **deep corridors** leading to grave chambers, cut some 26m deep into the hillside. Be sure to take a strong torch. At the very back is a well shaft of immense depth, which village tradition has it leads either to hell or to paradise, depending on which is more deserved.

**Dramatic cave tomb**

**Tricky climb**

At Kuruova a bumpy track to the right heads for the coast, winding 4km across the river bed and ploughed fields. Always bearing right when there is a choice, you will eventually reach the sea where the stones of the Middle Cypriot (c1800BC) fortress of **Nitovikla** stand a few courses high. It was excavated back in 1929. After wet weather the track is impassable for cars, as tractors gouge out great ruts which fill with water.

At the curious semi-troglodyte village of **Kaleburnu** (Greek Galinoporni), the tarmac stops. On the slope around it are many rock tombs, thought to have been originally Phoenician. On the outskirts, near the ruined church of **Ayia Anna**, is an extraordinary cave tomb 21m long.

**Semi-troglodyte village**

Returning to Ziyamet, you now continue on the main road to Yeni Erenköy (Greek Yialousa), the second largest town of the Karpas, with 2,500 inhabitants, the resettled Turkish Cypriots from the enclave of Erenköy (Kokkina) to the west. Beyond the

**Beaches**

pleasant rambling town, the road heads towards the coast, and some 2km from the edge of town a track to the left leads down to the Halk Plaj or **public beach**, a sandy bay with swings, changing cabins, and in the season, a barbecuing area offering snacks and kebabs.

One kilometre further on is the Karpaz Plaj, a simple but wholesome place offering fish, kebabs, and a **good sandy beach**. The beach could be kept cleaner, as a certain amount of rubbish and eel grass gets washed up.

*

**Ayia Trias**

After another 2 or 3km, the first tarmac road that forks to the right (inland) is unsignposted, but this is the road you take to reach Sipahi, the Greek village where the ruined church of **Ayia Trias** merits a short detour. As you enter the village look out for the old blue and red ex-school bus dumped on the right of the road. Beside it is the gate that leads across a path towards the ruined column stumps of the large early 5th century basilica. There is no guardian or entry fee. The setting is wonderfully pastoral, not to say overgrown, in the middle of orchards and fields, and sheep are frequently to be found grazing in the aisles. The site was excavated in the 1960s to reveal a large three-aisled structure. Few of the columns stand higher than head height, and the walls are rarely above waist height, but the memorable feature of the basilica is its mosaic floor paving. Open to the sky,

**Bucolic mosaics**

their colours, mainly reds, blues and whites, are faded, but the intricate geometric designs are striking, mixed in with patterns of foliage and the occasional Christian symbol. The north aisle shows two curious pairs of sandals facing in opposite directions (*see* back cover). The font can still be seen, and its cruciform shape is unique on the island.

**Traditional village**

The village of Sipahi (Greek Ayia Trias, Holy Trinity) still has 100 to 200 Greeks who chose to stay behind despite partition, and as you walk about in the village you will still see old men dressed in traditional rural baggy black trousers, and only Greek is spoken. Even in the times of mixed villages, Greeks and Turks always had separate schools and there was no official intermarriage between the communities. Today the non-Greek inhabitants are Turks from Trabzon and Samsun on the Black Sea.

Some 600 to 700 Greek Cypriots still live on the Karpas, the bulk of them in Dipkarpaz. Every Wednesday, the UN Peace Keeping Force in Cyprus, the 'Blue Berets', bring in about ten tons of food and **Resident** mail for them from Greek Nicosia. Relatives from the **Greek** Greek side are allowed to visit, though problems **community** sometimes occur. On one such visit recently, a Greek girl met and married a local Turk. The Greek Cypriots of Nicosia were outraged, convinced she had been abducted, and a band of friends marched on the Green Line in protest, demanding her return. A few months later, the girl returned to visit her parents in Nicosia, and stayed there. Her husband followed her, and was promptly deported by the Greek Cypriots. The numbers of this Greek community are, not surprisingly, slowly declining.

Some 8km (5 miles) east of Ayia Trias, back on the **Ayios** main Dipkarpaz road, you pass the derelict **Ayios** **Thrysos** **Thrysos** church on the left, with the **Florya restaurant** immediately opposite on the right. A simple lunch can be taken here, and it is possible, though not ideal, to swim from the rocky bay below. The restaurant also has ten simple but adequate rooms in a separate annexe. The 15th century church is whitewashed, with no frescoes, and empty except for a few wooden pews and the shell of the iconostasis. Lower down, close to the shore, is a smaller ruined medieval chapel, and beside it to the right is an even smaller cave church, probably Byzantine.

Some 3km further on, the observant may spot the isolated church of **Ayios Photios** uphill to the right, approached by a bad but driveable track. Thought to be 10th century, the church has no door, and inside **Rural** there are traces of frescoes showing figures on **church** horseback and a saint with a halo. Goat droppings form the major floor embellishment and the ceiling is adorned with swallows' nests.

Another 5km further east on the main road, is a rocky track leading inland just by a bridge over a dry stream bed. This brings you, after 2km of bumping,

**Abandoned monastery**

to an open clearing in the thick prickly scrubland. Here, abandoned, stands the monastery of **Panayia Eleousa**. The small 16th century whitewashed church has a decorated doorway, but inside the frescoes are covered in whitewash. Turks and Christians alike share the unfortunate habit of covering everything in whitewash. The monks' cells, looking of fairly recent build, stand in a row a little apart from the church. From here a track continues round in a loop to rejoin the main road a few kilometres further on.

The main road now begins a steep ascent up a fertile valley to reach Dipkarpaz, set on a hilltop. A lot of tobacco is grown in the area, and the soil's fertility is due to the abundance of wells, for the Karpas is rich in **underground water reservoirs**.

## FROM DIPKARPAZ TO THE TIP

**Dipkarpaz town**

The town of Dipkarpaz has little to delay the visitor today, except perhaps the petrol station. A few 18th century houses remain, but on the whole, the modern buildings are unmemorable. Set up on the hill to the left is the plain whitewashed church of **Ayios Synesius**, still used by the Greek community. The church stands on the site of the Orthodox cathedral which was built here in the 13th century when the

*Aphendrika basilica*

Greek Orthodox bishop was banished from Famagusta to Rizokarpaso by the Catholic Crusaders. The town has always been predominantly Greek, and you will notice a prevalence of blue or green eyes. Travellers of earlier centuries imagined the place filled with exotic beauties, but most modern visitors will search in vain.

## ** Ayios Philon

Beyond Dipkarpaz, to reach the northern coastline, you must turn left uphill from the centre of town, passing the long white school building on your left near the brow of the hill. You then pass under a derelict old archway, after which you fork left along the tarmac road to begin the long descent to the coast, 4km away.

**Seaside church**

As you make the descent you can already see in the distance the church of **Ayios Philon** standing alone on the shoreline. This was the site of the ancient city of Karpasia, founded by the legendary king Pygmalion of Cyprus. It was a flourishing Christian community until the Arab raiders burnt and sacked it in 802. Its inhabitants fled inland at that time and Rizokarpaso grew up.

The spot is beautifully lonely today, with only the sound of the sea against the rocks. The church is set on the cliffs above a rocky bay with three solitary palm trees breaking the skyline. Traces of the old harbour wall can still be seen where you swim, the large stone blocks still extending some 100m, while the remainder of the town lies hidden under the sand dunes away to the west. Philon was the name of the 5th century bishop who converted the inhabitants of the Karpas to Christianity. The well-preserved church complete with roof is 10th century, but beside it, open to the elements, the red, white and grey mosaic pavement and column remnants belong to a 5th century basilica, the original church of the bishop Philon. Nearby are a few heavily vandalised Greek houses of this century.

** **Aphendrika**

Beyond Ayios Philon an old dead-end tarmac road leads to Aphendrika in just 10 more minutes. There is no habitation at all on this stretch of coastline, and the tarmac turns into dirt track some 400m short of the ruined Christian settlement of Aphendrika, where the shells of **three churches** clustered together can still be **Deserted** easily explored. Silent except for the birdsong, the **trio** spot is utterly deserted.

In 200BC, Strabo the Greek historian tells us, Aphendrika was one of the six great cities of Cyprus, and the site is deceptively extensive. Apart from the three churches which date from the 12th and 14th centuries, you should also search for the citadel, set up on the hill east (inland) from the churches, with many of its rooms cut into the bedrock.

Walking towards the west, you will stumble on the **necropolis**, a whole area scattered with rock tombs, and the site of a **temple** beyond it. To the north, a **Scattered** 2km walk across the fields, lies the silted up **harbour** **city** of the ancient city, with a lonely sandy beach. The city has never been properly excavated.

From Aphendrika, the furthermost point of road on the north coast, it is 104km back to Kyrenia.

* **Towards Apostolos Andreas Monastery**

Returning to Dipkarpaz you now look out for the sign saying '**Zafer Burnu Manastırsı**' (Zafer Burnu being the name of the headland at the very tip of the island) which points to the left (south) from the centre of **The tip** town.

Scenically this stretch of isolated road along to the tip is the most magnificent on the island. There are no villages at all, and the only life you are likely to see is the occasional shepherd with his sheep and goats. Still dressed in last century's fashion of baggy **Pastoral** trousers, he is often spinning wool as he minds the **landscapes** flock. The bucolic landscape has an old world charm, and the gentle hills occasionally give way to magnificent vistas over huge sweeping bays. Scattered about all over the fields are fine buildings made from beautifully crafted stone. They look sufficiently grand to have been the residences of local mayors, but in fact they are simply storage barns and stables built by the former Greek inhabitants. Sometimes they even have crosses carved above the door.

As the road winds down through the hills from Dipkarpaz towards the sea, the landscape is covered in thick scrub. At certain seasons, the roadside is **Frenzied** thick with vehicles disgorging men wearing **hunting** camouflage gear, rifles and a glint in their eye. This is not, however, some relic of inter-communal strife, but the hunting season for birds. The hunters are legion, and as they quiver in the bushes, the chances of shooting each other must be quite high. The prey is mainly partridge and francolin, and the season, only on Sundays from November to January, is strictly controlled by the police. The sport is so popular that hunters travel all the way from Güzelyurt at the other end of the island for what is reckoned to be the best shooting. The catch is then taken home for eating. Cyprus is used by millions of birds as a stepping stone on their migrations between Europe and the Nile **Bird** Delta. The best bird watching spot for these migrants **watching** is at the **Gönyeli reservoir** on the northern edge of Nicosia.

Just where the road leaves the hunters in the hills and swoops round to the coast, you come to the **Blue Sea Hotel and Restaurant**, opened in 1989, in a lovely spot on a promontory a little above a beach and harbour. The proud new owner bought the building **Relaxing** which had been left unfinished by his Greek **hotel** predecessor. He has furnished it to a surprisingly high standard and his willing service makes a stop here very relaxing, either just for a meal or overnight (despite the lack of electricity).

The spot is known as **Khelones**, from the Greek for turtle, probably because turtles have always come here to lay their eggs in the sand. Behind the hotel is a ruined carob store and customs house, a relic of the days when carobs were exported, and the old harbour still remains below.

The road from here onwards stays more or less within sight of the coast, every corner bringing new

**Wild
beaches
and dunes**

panoramas over endless deserted bays. Most spectacular of all is one stretch some 4km before the monastery with an immense sandy beach and wild red sprawling dunes, reminiscent of Wales' Gower coast. Only rarely will you meet another car.

The road emerges suddenly at the monastery, arriving at a large open courtyard with one-roomed cells round the edge for pilgrims' accommodation. The current buildings date from 1867, though you could be forgiven for thinking them older as they are crumbling steadily and large black pigs seem to inhabit some of the rooms.

The monastery is also a **police post** and a pair of friendly policemen with a broken down jeep are based here. You must sign your name in their book and enter your passport number.

**Lourdes of
Cyprus**

The monastery has traditionally been the 'Lourdes' of Cyprus, with pilgrims coming from afar seeking cures for their afflictions. St Andrew was the great miracle worker and protector of travellers. Brother of Peter, and a fisherman like him, Andrew preached his mission in Greece and Turkey. On one such trip, the ship in which he was sailing ran out of drinking water, as they were passing Cyprus, so he told the one-eyed captain to put ashore here on the rocky headland. The sailors returned with water, and Andrew restored the captain's sight. The captain and

**Andrew's
miracle**

crew were converted and baptised by Andrew, and on his return trip the captain placed an icon of Andrew beside the wells. Hence the sanctity of the spot grew up. Andrew eventually settled in Patras on the Greek mainland, where he was crucified aged 80.

**Healing
waters**

The modern church beneath the bell tower is bare and unexciting, but beside an icon of the saint are hosts of **wax effigies** of people, children, limbs and even a cow, all seeking cures for long-term illnesses. Below the church, closer to the sea, is the **rock grotto** (the chapel was a 15th century addition) where you can still see the tiny spring of freshwater that Andrew is said to have endowed with special healing powers. Enough stories of cure exist to encourage the shrine to keep its reputation. A recent one tells of a paralysed

**Recent miracle**

girl whose parents reluctantly brought her here for the saint to effect a cure. They were both highly sceptical, but the girl insisted. It was late evening and she persuaded one of the monks to carry her into the rock chapel and leave her there. Two hours passed and the monk was suddenly startled by a cry. He turned to see the girl coming up the path on all fours at first, but then staggering weakly on her thin legs.

**The baptism business**

On Assumption Day, 15th August, and St Andrew's Day, 30th November, many pilgrims still come, Muslims and Christians alike, bringing offerings. Pre-1974 they would come on Sundays in their hundreds from Famagusta for family outings, and the priests were asked to perform so many baptisms that the font was fitted out with hot and cold taps. Numbers have dwindled somewhat since then. An old woman speaking Greek is generally to be found in the grotto, and she pulls back the curtains to show icons of the saint, expecting you to kiss them, and gives candles for you to light. The chapel walls are bare rock with no frescoes or decoration.

## Kastros

Having come all this way, if you still have a spare half hour you will probably want to complete your pilgrimage by driving the remaining 5km to the very tip of the island. The track is stony and bumpy but quite driveable in a saloon car, ending at the abandoned meteorological customs hut. It takes 15 to 20 minutes one way from the monastery, but though

**Cypriot Land's End**

the landscape is flat-ish, you cannot see the sea on both sides until the final 200m when the track approaches the bulbous rocky outcrop of Kastros. Scramble up to the summit of this rock for the best views of all.

A **Neolithic fort**, the oldest yet found on Cyprus along with Petra tou Limniti and Khirokhitia (c. 6000BC) was excavated on this summit in 1971-73, but only a few shapeless walls and foundations remain to the layman's eye.

Perched on the top, there is almost a climatic change, and the rock gives way to grass and lovely

**Picnic with Aphrodite and the gods**

white flowers, alive with butterflies and gentle wafts of breeze. **A temple of Aphrodite** once stood here to protect sailors from the treacherous rocks or to lure them in, according to her whim. If you have the energy to carry it to the summit, it is a wonderful spot for a picnic, here, at the end of the earth, lolling on the grass, gazing out at the string of little islands opposite, the Klides, the Keys of Cyprus, home only to the rare Audouin's Gull.

---

# THE GLOBETROTTERS CLUB

An international club which aims to share information on adventurous budget travel through monthly meetings and *Globe* magazine. Published every two months, *Globe* offers a wealth of information from reports of members' latest adventures to travel bargains and tips, plus the invaluable 'Mutual Aid' column where members can swap a house, sell a camper, find a travel companion or offer information on unusual places or hospitality to visiting members. London meetings are held monthly (Saturdays) and focus on a particular country or continent with illustrated talks.

*Enquiries to: Globetrotters Club, BCM/Roving, London WC1N 3XX.*

# Bradt Publications

## Travel Guides

41 Nortoft Road • Chalfont St Peter • Bucks • SL9 0LA • England  Fax/Telephone: 01494 873478

July 1995

Dear Reader

The future of tourism in North Cyprus hangs in the balance now as never before. Economic crises and political uncertainties grip the place, making life for residents, be they Turkish Cypriots or expatriates, difficult and frustrating. The right kind of tourism can be a lifeline for this struggling country. For North Cyprus the right kind is the older person (35+) who comes in search of the tranquillity lacking in other Mediterranean countries and who leaves the place as he found it. The chances are he will return many times. Needless to say I have a soft spot for North Cyprus - no one writes a guide like this for the money - and I do not want to see it ruined for my future holidays either!

Everyone has different impressions of a place and it is very valuable to have the views and experiences of others to balance my own. Do please continue to write and rest assured that your letters will get my personal attention.

Best wishes

# Appendix

# **Language**

**Think**
**backwards**

Turkish is a fiendishly difficult language for foreigners to become proficient in but, fortunately, English and German are widely understood. Its grammatical structure is unrelated to Indo-European and Romance languages and the major stumbling block to forming a sentence is the word order, which almost requires you to think 'backwards'. A sentence for example like 'The cake which I bought for you is on the table' retains the same shape in French, German, Spanish, Greek and even Arabic. In Turkish it becomes 'You-for buy-in-the-past-pertaining-to-me cake, table's surface-thereof-at is'. Not only is the order reversed, but the 12 English words become 6 in Turkish because of the Turkish habit of what is graphically called 'agglutinating', ie: sticking on extra words to the base word.

For those who would just like to have the bare minimum of vocabulary and expressions, the following list is given. Vowels and consonants are pronounced as in English and German except for:

the dotless i ('ı') which is peculiar to Turkish and is pronounced like the initial 'a' in 'away';

Turkish 'c' is pronounced as English 'j', so *cami* meaning mosque = jami, and Ercan airport = Erjan airport;

Turkish 'ç' is prounced as English 'ch', so Çamlıbel = Chamlibel;

Turkish 'ş' is pronounced as English 'sh', so Lefkoşa = Lefkosha;

Turkish 'ğ' is unpronounced at the end of a word, or in the middle of a word, so Gazimağosa = Gazima'osa.

## Everyday situations

| | |
|---|---|
| hello | *merhaba* |
| good morning /afternoon | *günaydın* or *iyi günler* |
| good evening | *iyi akşamlar* |
| goodbye (by person staying) | *güle güle* |
| goodbye (by person leaving) | *allaha ısmarladık* or *iyi günler* (lit 'good day') |
| yes | *evet* or *var* |
| no | *hayır* or *yok* |
| please | *lütfen* |
| thank you | *teşekkür ederim* |
| very nice, beautiful | *çok güzel* |
| how much is it? | *ne kadar?* |
| cheap | *ucuz* |
| expensive | *pahalı* |
| money | *para* |
| I have no money | *para yok* |
| shop | *dukkan* |
| open | *açık* |
| closed | *kapalı* |
| bank | *banka* |
| post office | *postane* |
| chemist/pharmacy | *eczane* |
| hospital | *hastahane* |
| police | *polis* |
| toilet | *tuvalet* |
| towel | *havlu* |
| soap | *sabun* |
| gents | *baylar* |
| ladies | *bayanlar* |
| room | *oda* |
| petrol | *benzin* |

# Food and drink

| | |
|---|---|
| breakfast | *kahvaltı* |
| eggs | *yumurta* |
| tea | *çay* |
| more tea | *daha çay* |
| coffee | *kahve* |
| milk | *süt* |
| sugar | *şeker* |
| bread | *ekmek* |
| butter | *tereyağ* |
| jam | *reçel* |
| honey | *bal* |
| cheese | *peynir* |
| soup | *corba* |
| salad | *salata* |
| fish | *balık* |
| chicken | *piliç* or *tavuk* |
| chips | *patates* |
| fruit | *meyva* |
| ice cream | *dondurma* |
| cake | *pasta* |
| water | *su* |
| mineral water | *maden suyu* |
| beer | *bira* |
| wine | *şarap* |
| red wine | *kırmızı şarap* |
| white wine | *beyaz şarap* |
| dry | *sek* |
| sweet | *tatlı* |
| the bill, please | *hesab, lütfen* |

The following words may often be seen on notices or street signs:

| | |
|---|---|
| to let/hire | *kıralık* |
| for sale | *satılık* |
| forbidden | *yasak* |
| forbidden zone | *yasak bölge* |
| military area | *askeri bölge* |
| road closed | *yol kapalı* |
| warning, watch out | *dikkat* |
| stop | *dur* |
| forest | *orman* |
| rubbish, waste | *çöp* |

# OLD AND NEW PLACE NAMES

| Current Turkish | Former Greek |
| --- | --- |
| Akçiçek | Sisklipos |
| Akdeniz | Ayia Irini |
| Akova | Gypsos |
| Alevkaya | Halevga |
| Alsancak | Karavas |
| Ardahan | Ardhana |
| Avtepe | Ayios Symeon |
| Bafra | Vokolidha |
| Bahceli | Kalogrea |
| Bellabayıs | Bellapais |
| Beşparmak | Pentadaktylos |
| Boğaz | Boghaz |
| Boğaztepe | Monarga |
| Boltaşlı | Lythrangomi |
| Çamlıbel | Myrtou |
| Çatalköy | Ayios Epiktitos |
| Çayırova | Ayios Theodhoros |
| Değirmenlik | Kythrea |
| Derince | Vathylakkas |
| Dikmen | Dhikomo |
| Dipkarpaz | Rizokarpaso |
| Edremit | Trimithi |
| Ercan | Tymbou |
| Erenköy | Kokkina |
| Erdenli | Tremetousha |
| Esentepe | Ayios Amvrosios |
| Gaziköy | Aphania |
| Gazimağosa | Famagusta |
| Geçitkale | Lefkoniko |
| Gemikonağı | Karavostasi |
| Girne | Kyrenia |
| Güngor | Koutsovendis |
| Gürpinar | Ayia Mani |
| Ilgaz | Phterykha |
| Güzelyurt | Morphou |
| Iskele | Trikomo |
| Kaleburnu | Galinoporni |
| Kalecık | Gastria |
| Kaplıca | Dhavlos |

| Current Turkish | Former Greek |
|---|---|
| Karaağaç | Kharcha |
| Karakum | Karakoumi |
| Karaoğlanoğlu | Ayios Yeoryios |
| Karaman | Karmi |
| Karğıyaka | Vasilia |
| Kayalar | Orga |
| Kaynakköy | Sykhari |
| Kırpasa | Karpas |
| Korucam | Kormakitis |
| Kuruova | Korovia |
| Lapta | Lapithos |
| Lefke | Lefka |
| Lefkoşa | Nicosia |
| Malatya | Paleosophos |
| Maraş | Varosha |
| Mutluyaka | Styllos |
| Ozanköy | Kazaphani |
| Pasaköy | Asha |
| Sazlıköy | Lavidhia |
| Şehitler | Sandlaris |
| Sınırüstü | Syngrasis |
| Sipahi | Ayia Trias |
| Şirinevler | Ayios Ermolaos |
| Taşkent | Vouno |
| Tatlısu | Akanthou |
| Tepebaşı | Dhiorios |
| Tirmen | Trypimeni |
| Turunçlu | Strongylos |
| Turnalar | Yerani |
| Tuzla | Engomi |
| Yedidalga | Potamos tou Kambou |
| Yeni Erenköy | Yialousa |
| Yıldırım | Milea |
| Yılmazköy | Skylloura |
| Zafer Burnu | Cape Apostolos Andreas |
| Zeytin Burnu | Cape Elea |
| Ziyamet | Leonarisso |

# FURTHER READING

Dodd, Clement H:
*The Cyprus Issue*, Eothen Press 1994.
*The Political, Social and Economic Development of Northern Cyprus*, Eothen Press 1993.

Durrell, Lawrence *Bitter Lemons* Faber & Faber 1957. Entertaining and moving account of his years at Bellapais from 1953 to 1956.

Gunnis, Rupert *Historic Cyprus* London 1936, republished Lefkoşa 1973. Architectural description of all the churches and monuments on the island.

Halliday, Sonia and Lushington, Lara *High above Kıbrıs* Angus Hudson Ltd 1985. Coffee-table book with many splendid photos.

Home, Gordon *Cyprus then and now* J M Dent & Sons 1960. Good for historical background before partition.

Luke, Sir Harry *Cyprus under the Turks 1571-1878* Hurst 1971. Interesting historical account based on British consular archives.

Oberling, Pierre *The Road to Bellapais* Columbia University Press 1982. Account of intercommunal strife and events leading up to partition.

Reddaway, John *Burdened with Cyprus — the British Connection* Weidenfeld & Nicolson 1987. Readable account of Britain's involvement with Cyprus from 1878 onwards. Reddaway was Administrative Secretary in the British Embassy in Nicosia during the EOKA period.

Thubron, Colin *Journey into Cyprus* Heinemann 1975. Fascinating description of his 600-mile walk through the island in 1972.

Volcan, Vamik D and Itzkowitz, Norman *Turks and Greeks Neighbours in Conflict* Eothen Press 1995.

## Flora, fauna and walks
The following reference material will be of particular interest:

Flint, P and Stewart, P *The Birds of Cyprus: An annotated check list.* £22.50.

Halliday, Sonia and Lushington, Lara *Flowers of North Cyprus* Angus Hudson Ltd 1988.

Meikle, R D *The Flora of Cyprus*. Two volumes, £25 and £40.

Oddie, B and Moore, D *A Birdwatcher's Guide to the Birds of Cyprus.* £5.95

Pantelas, V and Papachristophorou, T *Cyprus Flora in Colour: the Endemics*. £12.50.

Took, J M E *Birds of Cyprus*. £9.95.

# MEASUREMENTS AND CONVERSIONS

| To convert | Multiply by | To convert | Multiply by |
|---|---|---|---|
| Inches to centimetres | 2.54 | US gallons to litres | 3.785 |
| Centimetres to inches | 0.3937 | Litres to US gallons | 0.264 |
| Feet to metres | 0.3048 | Ounces to grams | 28.35 |
| Metres to feet | 3.281 | Grams to ounces | 0.03527 |
| Yards to metres | 0.9144 | Pounds to grams | 453.6 |
| Metres to yards | 1.094 | Grams to pounds | 0.002205 |
| Miles to kilometres | 1.609 | Pounds to kilograms | 0.4536 |
| Kilometres to miles | 0.6214 | Kilograms to pounds | 2.205 |
| Acres to hectares | 0.4047 | British tons to kilograms | 1016.0 |
| Hectares to acres | 2.471 | Kilograms to British tons | 0.0009842 |
| Imperial gallons to litres | 4.546 | US tons to kilograms | 907.0 |
| Litres to imperial gallons | 0.22 | Kilograms to US tons | 0.000907 |

(5 imperial gallons are equal to 6 US gallons.
A British ton is 2,240 lbs. A US ton is 2,000 lbs.)

# Temperature conversion table

The bold figures in the central columns can be read as either centigrade or fahrenheit

| Centigrade | | Fahrenheit | Centigrade | | Fahrenheit |
|---|---|---|---|---|---|
| -18 | **0** | 32 | 10 | **50** | 122 |
| -15 | **5** | 41 | 13 | **55** | 131 |
| -12 | **10** | 50 | 16 | **60** | 140 |
| - 9 | **15** | 59 | 18 | **65** | 149 |
| - 7 | **20** | 68 | 21 | **70** | 158 |
| - 4 | **25** | 77 | 24 | **75** | 167 |
| - 1 | **30** | 86 | 27 | **80** | 176 |
| 2 | **35** | 95 | 32 | **90** | 194 |
| 4 | **40** | 104 | 38 | **100** | 212 |
| 7 | **45** | 113 | 40 | **104** | |

# NOTES

# NOTES

# NOTES

# INDEX